DUP

Beyond
Charlottesville

Beyond Charlottesville

TAKING A STAND AGAINST
WHITE NATIONALISM

...

Terry McAuliffe

THOMAS DUNNE BOOKS ⚏ ST. MARTIN'S PRESS
NEW YORK

First published in the United States by Thomas Dunne Books,
an imprint of the St. Martin's Publishing Group

BEYOND CHARLOTTESVILLE. Copyright © 2019 by Terry McAuliffe.
Foreword copyright @ by John Lewis. All rights reserved. Printed in the
United States of America. For information, address
St. Martin's Publishing Group, 120 Broadway, New York, NY 10271.

Designed by Steven Seighman

The Library of Congress Cataloging-in-Publication Data
is available upon request.

ISBN: 978-1-250-24588-5 (hardcover)
ISBN: 978-1-250-24587-8 (ebook)

Our books may be purchased in bulk for promotional, educational,
or business use. Please contact your local bookseller or the Macmillan
Corporate and Premium Sales Department at 1-800-221-7945, extension
5442, or by email at MacmillanSpecialMarkets@macmillan.com.

First Edition: July 2019

10 9 8 7 6 5 4 3 2 1

I dedicate this book to Heather Heyer, Jay Cullen, and Berke Bates,
who were all killed on August 12, 2017, doing what they loved.

Contents

...

Foreword

BY Congressman John Lewis

■ ■ ■

I t made me very sad to see what happened in Charlottesville, Virginia, in August 2017 when a thousand white nationalists and Ku Klux Klan followers showed up in broad daylight to preach violence and hate. I have been working against hate and resisting violence for more than half a century, and I thought we had come much farther as a people, as a nation. To me, August 12, 2017, was a very dark hour, a dark period for America. It hurt me to see so many people engaging in this type of madness.

The madness continued when the president of the United States stepped in front of the microphones that dark day and said he was condemning the tragic events of Charlottesville as "an egregious display of hatred, bigotry, and violence on many sides, on many sides." That was very surprising to me, that any person in a position of leadership would equate the actions of violent white nationalists with those of peaceful protesters. People came to Charlottesville from all over the country preaching hate, division, and separation, and were met by a principled stand of locals who turned out to protest hate, often linking arms in nonviolent protest. That reminded me of the way my brothers and sisters and I had linked arms in Selma, Alabama, in 1965 and tried to cross the Edmund Pettus Bridge, named for a Confederate general, and were beaten, tear-gassed, trampled by horses, and left bloody.

I always believe in hope, and finally, on the dark day of the Charlottesville tragedy in August 2017, I had cause for hope. My heart lifted that day when at last someone spoke the words that needed to be spoken. Someone stood up and showed the leadership that the people of Charlottesville, the people of the entire nation, required in that dark hour to begin to steer toward the light. My friend Governor Terry McAuliffe was strong and clear in his condemnation of hate and racism.

"To all the white supremacists and the Nazis who came into Charlottesville today, our message is plain and simple: Go home. You are not wanted in this great commonwealth. Shame on you," the governor said that day. "You came here today to hurt people and you did hurt people. But my message is clear: We are stronger than you. You have made our commonwealth stronger. You will not succeed. There is no place for you here, there is no place for you in America."

Governor McAuliffe spoke the truth that day. He came across with conviction. Anyone listening could see he was speaking from the heart, angry and sad but filled with a sense of purpose.

"I cried when I heard your speech," I told the governor the following Monday when I called him to thank him for his leadership. "That was one of the great speeches I've ever heard in my life."

"Thank you, Congressman," he said. "Coming from you, that's an incredible compliment."

Terry McAuliffe is not one to be at a loss for words, but that compliment left him momentarily speechless. It's true, I've had the privilege to hear many great speeches in my lifetime, most especially during the March on Washington in August 1963 that I helped organize. I was one of ten speakers that day standing near the Lincoln Memorial, the last of whom was my friend, the Reverend Martin Luther King Jr., who that day delivered his timeless "I Have a Dream" speech.

Charlottesville chilled me to my bones because I had honestly believed we had come far enough as a country not to have to witness such naked hatred and racism on such a scale in broad daylight again. We always knew our struggle against hatred and racism would be a long one. We have lost so many brothers and sisters along the way. I'm the only speaker from the March on Washington in August 1963 who is still alive. We must honor the memory of those we have lost by remembering. It's a constant struggle. We can never rest. We can never be weary, but must continue always to find a way to get in the way of racism and hatred.

Earlier this year, I visited the Sixteenth Street Baptist Church in Birmingham, Alabama, the church where four girls were killed by Ku Klux Klan domestic terrorists on a Sunday morning, September 15, 1963. Addie Mae Collins, Cynthia Wesley, and Carole Robertson were each fourteen years old, and Carol Denise McNair was just eleven. When I visited the church, a group of high school students presented a play telling the story of what happened in 1963, and how it happened, both for members of Congress and for young people. I wish every American could see and witness this play. We're going to try to bring it to Washington, maybe on Capitol Hill, or the Kennedy Center. These young people were black, they were white, they were Latino, they were Asian American, and their play made us cry and it made us laugh. That's progress.

Over the years, I have often been subjected to physical harm, and I bear the scars of the struggle, a small price to pay for playing my part to march us forward toward progress and understanding. Nashville was the first major city in the South to desegregate lunch counters and movie theaters, and in Nashville we learned the philosophy and the discipline of nonviolence from

Jim Lawson, who had traveled to India as a Methodist minister and studied the teachings of Mahatma Gandhi. As I wrote in my memoir, *Walking With the Wind*: "I couldn't have found a better teacher than Jim Lawson. . . . There was something of a mystic about him, something holy, so gathered, about his manner, the way he had of leaning back in his chair and listening, really *listening*. . . . We discussed and debated every aspect of Gandhi's principles, from his concept of *ahimsa*—the Hindu idea of nonviolent passive resistance—to *satyagraha*—literally, 'steadfastness in truth,' a grounding foundation of nonviolent civil disobedience, of active pacifism."

In 1961, the same year Barack Obama was born, black and white people could not board a Greyhound bus and be seated together. We used the principles of nonviolent civil disobedience Jim had taught us that year to work for change through the Freedom Rides, which I planned as an organizer of the Student Nonviolent Coordinating Committee. It was black and white together on long bus rides into the South, no matter the consequences. At a stop in Rock Hill, South Carolina, I tried to enter a so-called white waiting room and was attacked by members of the KKK, beaten, and left in a pool of blood.

Remarkably, a man named Elwin Wilson, one of the Klansmen who attacked me that day in South Carolina, visited me in my Capitol Hill office in 2009, along with his son.

"Mr. Lewis, I'm one of the people that beat you," he told me. "I want to apologize. Will you forgive me?"

Elwin Wilson and his son were both in tears.

"I forgive you," I told the man.

You always like to think that we've come a distance and made progress as a nation, which was how I felt when a former KKK member like Elwin Wilson would pay me a visit in the United States Capitol to offer a heartfelt apology in the presence of his son. Then to have people come along to attempt to destroy that sense of progress, that sense of hope, the way they did in Charlottesville with a return of the KKK; it showed me, as it showed the entire country, how very long a way we still have to go.

We will get there. There may be some more ups and downs, and people of my generation may not be there to see the day, but as a nation, as a people, we will get there. We've got to teach people not to be afraid. We have to reach out to young people, to young children, and remind them that we are one people, we are one family, we are all in one house—the American house—but it's not just the American house, it's the world house.

The answer to hate is not more hate, it's love. As Dr. King said in his "Where Do We Go from Here?" speech in 1967: "I have seen too much hate. I've seen too much hate on the faces of sheriffs in the South. I've seen hate on the faces of too many Klansmen. . . . I say to myself that hate is too great a burden to bear. I have decided to love. If you are seeking the highest good, I think you can find it through love."

You have to lay down your hate, lay it down and respect the dignity and the worth of every human being. It's painful when a national tragedy like Charlottesville slows down the movement to free and liberate our society. When something like this comes along, it arrests that movement, it delays the hopes and dreams and aspirations of our people, but it can never stop us. We just have to work harder.

Throughout our country there's still a deep sickness, and there are forces that like to stir it up and bring it to this other level. We've got to speak the truth, to remind people of who we are and where we've been. We have to be tireless in working to build what Dr. King called "the beloved community," to try to redeem the soul of America.

That's why every March I take people back to Montgomery, to Birmingham, to Selma for a Civil Rights Pilgrimage. Dozens of members of Congress come to Alabama and visit the Sixteenth

Street Baptist Church, the Edmund Pettus Bridge, the Rosa Parks Bus Site, and other key locations. I think when people go there it tends to have a cleansing effect. Members tell me afterward they will never, ever be the same.

That's also why I spend time talking to young people. They know what they need to do. Young people get it. We don't come into this world discriminating against another person because of their race or their color, or because they may be from some other land; we come into this world clean and free. People are taught. They pick things up from the adults. Our environment, our friends, our parents, or the school we attend tells us that we are different and should see other people as different.

Some people put up a billboard in Pennsylvania that accused me of being a racist. I said there's not a racist hair on my head and not a racist bone in my body. There never has been and never will be. We've got to teach people just to be human. I don't look at someone as being black or white. They're just human.

The story of Charlottesville needs to be told again and again, as in this powerful, important book from Terry McAuliffe, which I can't recommend highly enough. It is a must for all of us to stay engaged, so that the lessons of that dark day for America can never be forgotten and can always serve to educate and inform. The future of our society, the future of America, is with the young. But old people like myself, we can encourage the young. We're never too young or too old to make a contribution. If we're going to have a future as a nation, and as a people, we all must be engaged, we all must be involved in some way, helping to deal with the local community, helping to redeem the soul of America. We must do it. We don't have a choice. We have a national problem with hate and fear and racism. It's like a raging fire burning that can consume us all. That's why we must stop the burning. We must quench the flames and look to the future.

Saturday Afternoon, August 12, 2017

. . .

When I hung up with President Trump that day, there was no question in my mind that he was going to do the right thing. Foolish me, I was convinced that he was going to clearly condemn the white supremacists and neo-Nazis who had come out of the shadows to march through the streets of Charlottesville, Virginia, in broad daylight, armed and dangerous, screaming some of the most obscene, sickening language I've ever heard in my life. It was a national tragedy, what unfolded that weekend in Virginia. During our short call, I briefed the president on the dangerous situation we'd been confronting on the ground in Charlottesville. I'd declared a state of emergency late that morning and we cleared the protesters from the park, but it remained a volatile mix. I told the president that these were dangerous people who had invaded Charlottesville that weekend, coming from all over the country.

"This is a really important moment in our history, Mr. President," I said.

Look, I'd known Donald Trump for years. I'd golfed with him,

I'd dined with him, and as governor of Virginia and chair of the National Governors Association, I'd dealt with him often during his presidency. I had no illusions that a guy whose favorite thing to do was watch himself on TV was suddenly going to turn into Bobby Kennedy. Eloquence was no more his thing than consistency. But in the middle of a crisis like this, I honestly did expect him to rise to the occasion. That's what presidents do.

I truly believed that this president of the United States, like other presidents before him, was about to show that he could grow in office. We saw that with President Clinton after Oklahoma City. We saw it with President Bush after 9/11. And we saw it with President Obama after Charleston, South Carolina. When those three presidents addressed the nation in times of tragedy, it didn't matter if they were Democrat or Republican, young or old, white or black. It didn't even matter if they were eloquent or tongue-tied, sweeping or measured, flowery or plainspoken; it just mattered that they found a way to sound humble and sincere in appealing to the greater good in all of us.

Donald Trump gave me every reason to believe he was just about to do that. He said he would be going in front of the cameras right after our call for a news conference at his golf course in New Jersey to address the tragedy of what happened in Charlottesville. I would hold off on making any statement until after the president had spoken. He was going to come out against these white supremacists brandishing Confederate flags and neo-Nazis with swastikas on their shields. This should not have been a hard choice to make. Trump was going to take a clear stand. I thanked the president for his support in our time of crisis and said, "Mr. President, let's you and I work together to heal these wounds."

Then something happened. I don't know what, but something. I kept waiting, and still there was no Trump press conference. An hour later, still no Trump. He had just talked to me, the governor of Virginia, and I had given him updated information from all the relevant law enforcement on the ground in Charlottesville. The nation was waiting. Who else did he need to consult? I can't say. I can't account for the missing hours. I'm sure we'll read later in someone's memoir about how one of the ideologues in the White House cornered the president and told him he couldn't alienate the hard-core racists. That would be at odds with their strategic political game plan. I just know that when Trump finally stepped up to the podium, he let America down.

"We condemn in the strongest possible terms this egregious display of hatred, bigotry, and violence," he began, but then added, looking up from his notes, "on many sides, on many sides."

What was he talking about? On *many* sides? The president and I had only talked about one side, the side with the heavily armed white supremacists and neo-Nazis on a mission of hate and violence, not the other side with peaceful protesters taking a stand against hate and division. I was flabbergasted to hear Trump pulling his all-sides-are-to-blame nonsense. I was shocked, I felt our nation had just been sucker punched. How could he not even utter the words "white supremacist" or "neo-Nazi" in describing what had happened in Charlottesville?

Talk about throwing a lit match into a pool of gasoline. In Virginia we were doing everything we could to keep people safe and turn the temperature down on this volatile mess, and here was the president of the United States egging on these hate-filled extremists and infuriating everyone else. The only way to deal with this situation was to state the stark truth of what had happened and what it meant. Listening to the president's brief remarks, even before he'd finished, I knew what I had to do.

You know the really sad part? Parts of Trump's short speech that day were actually on point. "I just got off the phone with the governor of Virginia, Terry McAuliffe, and we agree that the hate and the division must stop, and must stop right now," he said. "We have to come together as Americans with love for our nation and true affection—really, I say this so strongly, true affection for each other."

It's hard to believe those words actually came out of Donald Trump's mouth.

"We have so many incredible things happening in our country, so when I watch Charlottesville, to me it's very, very sad," Trump said. "Above all else, we must remember this truth: No matter our color, creed, religion, or political party, we are all Americans first."

His staff had given him the words to sound presidential, the words to bring the country together. Instead, Donald Trump chose that day to come out as a white supremacist. He chose that day to come out as a dyed-in-the-wool, unapologetic racist. It was his coming-out party that day; no more room for any doubt that this man was at heart a racist and a hater.

Even a lot of leading Republicans, who had covered for Trump during his campaign when he repeatedly made openly racist appeals, condemned Trump's bizarre remarks that day as an endorsement of racism and hate.

Senator Orrin Hatch: "We should call evil by its name. My brother didn't give his life fighting Hitler for Nazi ideas to go unchallenged here at home."

House Speaker Paul Ryan: "White supremacy is a scourge. This hate and its terrorism must be confronted and defeated."

Marco Rubio even dubbed it "a terror attack" by white supremacists—and called on the president to describe events for what they were. A terrorist used his car as a weapon and killed thirty-two-year-old Heather Heyer. What was she doing at the time? Peacefully protesting. There was no room for moral equivalence here, and the nation recoiled in outrage and shock.

As the governor of Virginia, I knew I needed to speak out. Just before I went out to deliver my remarks, we received the devastating news that Trooper 1, the Virginia State Police helicopter assigned to me, had crashed on a surveillance mission during the chaos. We lost both Virginia state trooper pilots, Lieutenant Jay Cullen and Trooper Pilot Berke Bates. Jay was my regular pilot and led our State Police Aviation Unit, and Berke, a newly minted pilot, had been on my Executive Protection Unit (EPU), which made him like a member of my family.

I was crushed. I stepped up to the podium determined to keep my cool, but I was filled with sadness and seething with anger, and I was not about to hide it.

"I have a message to all the white supremacists and the Nazis who came into Charlottesville today," I said. "Our message is plain and simple: Go home and never come back. You are not wanted in this great commonwealth. Shame on you. You pretend that you are patriots, but you are anything but a patriot. You are a bunch of cowards. You want to talk about patriots, talk about Thomas Jefferson and George Washington, who brought our country together. Think about the patriots today, the young men and women who are wearing the cloth of our country. Somewhere around the globe they are putting their life in danger."

I didn't mention that my oldest son, Jack, was a United States Marine deployed in Iraq at the time. In fact, Berke had recently called to tell me that he had just sent Jack a care package with cigars and a bottle of Irish whiskey disguised in a bottle of Listerine, but of course the package was examined by military inspectors. The cigars reached Jack. The whiskey didn't.

"They are patriots," I said. "You are not. You came here today to hurt people. And you did hurt people. My message is clear: We are stronger than you. You have made our commonwealth stronger. You will not succeed. There is no place for you here, there is no place for you in America."

When I think back on that weekend, President Trump did make one valid point in his "on many sides" speech, no matter how hollow the words sounded that day. "We want to get the situation straightened out in Charlottesville, and we want to study it," he said. "And we want to see what we're doing wrong as a country where things like this can happen."

Yes, we do need to study that weekend. We do need to study the forces and actions that enable such horrible, white supremacist violence—out in the open, not under a white hood, not under the cover of night, but marching right down our streets in the full glare of daylight. We need to study and remember and fight racism, together. That's why I'm writing this book.

As these events were unfolding in August 2017 I didn't have a lot of time for deep reflection. I was busy being governor. After leaving office, it seemed like every day someone wanted to talk to me about Charlottesville. I couldn't stop thinking about everything that had happened and what it meant to our country. I knew I was still looking for answers and perspective, and figured if I was, others were as well. If I don't go back over it now, and get it down right, in detail, I worry that so much of what happened will be lost. I can't let that happen. I can't be quiet on this one, any more than I was quiet that Saturday. I will take you through the tragic events of that weekend. As difficult as that will be for many readers, to move beyond Charlottesville that is the work that is required of us. Finishing this book, in March 2019, the shock of that weekend in Charlottesville still feels raw. Remembering is one way to honor the memory of Heather Heyer and Jay and Berke. I dedicate this book to those three and to everyone everywhere who has been harmed by the evil of racism.

CHAPTER 1

A Virginian by Choice

. . .

P eople go into politics for a lot of different reasons. I've pretty much seen it all since 1979 when I went to work on Jimmy Carter's presidential reelection campaign. For me politics was always in my blood. It wasn't any more complicated than that. Both of my parents were gregarious, friendly people who saw it as their job to make a difference for other people. Both of them loved being in a room full of strangers, meeting new people and hearing their stories. That's always been me. I can't hide who I am and never have tried. I love people and I could care less whether the person I'm talking to is a ticket taker in a movie theater, a truck driver, a school principal, or a head of state or captain of industry—they all have a story to tell. And I'll never get tired of listening to people tell those stories. I always learn something.

You know what else? I have a lot of energy. Sleep when you're dead, I've been saying for years. I love people, I love ideas, and I love life. If you want to be in the middle of the action, using good ideas to help peoples' lives change for the better, then you want to be the one in charge, like a governor, able to show executive leadership and thoughtful planning and cool decision-making under pressure.

Running for political office has its ups and downs. Running for Virginia governor in 2009, I had to smile my way through many a tense meeting where my "Yankee" background had people wondering if they ought to listen to a single word I said. I never let that faze me. I kept talking to people—and kept listening. I told Virginia voters about my plans for the future, and they listened. You know why? Because when I talked about jobs, jobs, jobs, they saw the fire in my eyes and heard the conviction in my voice. They believed I would work my tail off to bring investment to Virginia and create good-paying jobs all over the state. I was always going to run as an advocate for jobs because as a born businessman and entrepreneur, I knew that was in my wheelhouse, and I knew that honest, good-paying jobs were what people cared most about. If I was talking about jobs with people, I knew I was on solid footing.

Other issues were more challenging, especially that of the racial divide. I'm a problem solver, happiest when I can bring people together and we can roll up our sleeves and get to work forming a bold plan to tackle a problem, and then putting that into action. That approach does not lend itself to fighting racism and its legacies. I knew I had a lot to learn about just how deep those legacies ran. Richmond, Virginia, had been the capital of the Confederacy, spearheading the resistance to freeing slaves in the Civil War. I remember my traveling chief of staff in 2009, Justin Paschal, pointing out all the Confederate statues and monuments we kept seeing as we traveled the state.

Early in the campaign, I had an event near Harrisonburg in the Shenandoah Valley. As I was speaking, a woman approached Justin, who is African American.

"Do you know where you are?" she asked him.

He didn't like where this was going, but what could he say? "Yes," he replied.

"Well, you should know that we had a Klan rally here last weekend," she said. "I'd be careful if I were you."

I was shocked when Justin later told me what she'd said. In all honesty, I hadn't heard about the Ku Klux Klan in years. I couldn't stop talking about that for weeks. Another time, Justin and I were heading into an event and at the door they were giving everyone a Confederate flag sticker. Justin was with me and they tried to put one of those stickers on his lapel. "You do that, I'll break your arm," he said.

My wife, Dorothy, will never forget walking through the crowd at a political event with Justin right beside her when a man suddenly came up to her and said, "I would *never* vote for your husband. He's a n— lover." She was horrified.

Those were eye-popping moments, but they were also isolated incidents. You didn't want to fall into stereotypes and assume people were racists just because a fringe element had hung on to centuries-old hatreds.

Even people in Virginia who liked me as a candidate thought I might have a hard time convincing Virginians I was truly one of them. Larry J. Sabato, the University of Virginia political guru, told me in 2009 when I went down to see him in Charlottesville that he thought I'd picked the wrong state. For years there had been chatter that I might run for governor, and people kept guessing different states.

"I thought you lived in New York," Larry told me.

New York? I hadn't lived in New York since the 1970s when I left for college. Florida? I was proud I'd taken over a bankrupt company and built it into one of the largest home-building companies in the state, constructing more than six thousand homes, but for me Florida was where I went on vacation or to visit my father-in-law, Richard Swann. The fact was, Virginia was my home, where I paid taxes and sent my children to school. I wanted to lead my home state.

"My lasting impression of Terry was that he had enormous energy, maybe a ridiculous amount of energy," Larry said later. "And that he was tough. Real politics isn't political science. It's what you instinctively know about people and how they vote. . . . He could throw a good punch and take one, too. A lot of politicians have glass jaws. Not Terry."

I knew when I first decided to run for governor of Virginia it wasn't going to be easy. There were a few obstacles to overcome, starting with the fact that I'd never run for public office before, unless you count chairman of the Democratic National Committee. It was a gutsy move to run, no question. But my whole life from when I was a kid growing up in Syracuse, New York, starting my own driveway-paving company when I was fourteen, had been all about working hard, paying close attention to what people actually want and need, and having fun doing it. So when I ran for governor of the commonwealth in 2009 I was running to win and running to make a difference. You can't do that finishing second.

Dorothy and I first settled down in Virginia back in 1992, soon after our first child, Dori, was born. We wanted a house with a backyard where the kids could run around and play with the dogs. We'd both attended college and law school in Washington, DC, and had been in the area for years already. We chose McLean, Virginia, as the place we wanted to put down roots, and we raised our family of five children there. As Dorothy liked to say, by 2009 she'd shopped at the same Safeway grocery store for seventeen years.

Did that make us Virginians? It depended on who you asked. Northern Virginia, where we lived, was full of people who had come from somewhere else. Other parts of the state were a different story. Some folks figured you had to be fourth- or fifth-generation to be considered a true Virginian and I was OK with that. As I used to say on the campaign trail, I didn't have any choice of where I was born. My mother made that decision for me. But when I had to make my own decision, I chose Virginia.

I was obviously aware it would raise some eyebrows when I announced in January 2009 that I was running for governor of Virginia. I got it. People knew me for my work in national politics. They'd seen me on TV as DNC chairman, talking issues—or politics—with various Republican counterparts. What they didn't know, at least not at first, was why I was running for governor and how sure I was that I could transform the state, bring it into the twenty-first century, and build a dynamic new economy.

It's funny about politics. People are always going to pigeonhole you. They always try to figure out an election that's coming up by studying what happened in the election before. I'm not sure how helpful any of that is. I've always tried to go out and fight for what I believe, focusing on getting results, and at the same time, trying to show that politics doesn't have to be boring. You can be serious and committed and still try to stir things up and make even a routine event fun and interesting, especially if you love what you're doing when you're giving speeches or meeting voters or even debating your opponents.

I'm known for my perpetual optimism. Until I published my first book in 2007, the *New York Times* bestseller *What a Party!*, a lot of people assumed that anyone having as much fun as I was couldn't also be serious, very serious, about doing the work of making a difference for people and governing a state of eight and a half million people.

I used to kid Marc Fisher, the *Washington Post* columnist, about his November 2008 column assuring readers that, as the headline put it, GUBERNATORIAL IS ONE THING TERRY MCAULIFFE ISN'T. Again, he was mostly writing about my image, but it's funny what he chose to mention. "McAuliffe wants to be governor of Virginia, a job that has more to do with repairing roads and managing prisons than it does with sweet-talking Hollywood moguls and spinning the loudmouths on CNN, MSNBC and Fox," Fisher wrote. "Could a state in a grim budget situation use a chief executive who once wrestled a 280-pound alligator to land a $15,000 donation from a Florida Indian tribe?"

I didn't get that one. How does wrestling an alligator thirty years before disqualify you from serving the people of the commonwealth? There are probably worse ways to prepare for the challenge of working with the Virginia General Assembly. I'm kidding.

My main challenger for the Democratic nomination, or so I assumed, was Brian Moran, not the more conservative Democratic candidate Creigh Deeds. Like me, Brian came from an Irish family with an interest in politics, and his brother, Jim Moran, was a longtime congressman representing Northern Virginia. Like me, Brian was originally from the Northeast, and, like me, he loves to talk. A couple of years earlier he'd had me come and speak at his annual pancake breakfast fund-raiser. He joked that if the morning coffee didn't wake everyone up, listening to me sure did.

"Both of us would speak at a high decibel level and get people pumped up, almost like a football coach," Brian says now. "My dad was a football coach. You wanted to inspire people and get them fired up, and Terry did that on steroids."

We weren't both going to win the nomination for governor. Brian had been in Virginia politics for years, having served in the House of Delegates since 1996 and as Democratic caucus chairman, and he saw me as a latecomer to the race. He and I were both going after Northern Virginians especially; that was going to be our prime territory, and he was pretty tough on me that year.

"There is no reason to perceive him as a Virginia Democrat,"

Brian told one reporter that year. "Before the last six months, he's had little, if any, involvement not only in Virginia politics but in Virginia governance."

I expected Brian to throw a few elbows my way—that's politics, and none of it ever bothered me, but Brian went a bit overboard. His campaign advisers had him all jacked up to go after me as much as he could. We had Virginia's annual state fund-raising dinner in February 2009, headlined by President Bill Clinton, who came as a favor to me, featuring all three candidates. Brian spent all his time taking shots at me. As *The Washington Post* put it, "Moran took repeated swipes. . . . Some Democrats called it inappropriate to criticize a fellow Democrat at a party event."

I'd made a pledge not to attack either of my primary opponents, and I stuck to that. Brian hit me hard on the stump and in our debates, but his early lead in a couple of polls faded and I was ahead in five straight polls from April to May with Creigh Deeds a distant third. *The New York Times Magazine* sent out a veteran political reporter, Adam Nagourney, to report on how I was doing as a candidate, and we had some fun challenging Adam to try to keep up with me. (He couldn't.)

I had "outtalked, out-handshook, outspent, outhustled, outshouted and just plain outcampaigned them across Richmond," Nagourney wrote. "McAuliffe, tipping back bottles of beer, stayed so late talking to party members at the Virginia Young Democrats reception—he made sure I noted he was there an hour longer than Moran or Deeds—that it seemed just a matter of time until the cleanup crew swept him out with a broom."

Then on May 22 came a political earthquake. *The Washington Post* weighed in with its editorial making an endorsement, and for some reason decided to throw its weight behind Creigh Deeds. Keep in mind, at that point every poll for the last couple of months had me up by at least nine percentage points. My problem with the *Post* editorial wasn't so much the argument for Deeds. What bothered me was the use of one word that changed everything. A May 3 feature in *The Post* had included the bizarre assertion that I'd referred to myself as a "huckster" in my own autobiography. Not true. The reporter who wrote that article could have spent five minutes checking the facts with a simple Amazon search, and realized that no, that word does not occur once in the more than one hundred thousand words of my first book.

But the *Post* editorial repeated the "huckster" claim. Not until May 27, less than two weeks before the Democratic primary, did we get a correction printed. The reference in my book was to my Uncle Billy Byrne admiringly calling me a "young hustler" when I started my paving business at age fourteen. He loved my gumption in going out and getting an old milk truck that belonged to him running, and driving it home, even though I was too young to have a driver's license at the time, and painting McAuliffe Driveway Maintenance on the side. What can I say? I was a born entrepreneur.

After that *Post* editorial, my lead in the polls evaporated, and Deeds went on to win the nomination, with me coming in a distant second—then he lost the general election to the Republican, Bob McDonnell, 58.6% to 41.2%. Some people who didn't know me thought I might "fade back into national politics" after that, as Larry Sabato put it, but I'm not one to fade, and I wanted to make a difference in Virginia. I took some time to ask what we could have done better in the '09 campaign, and then I got to work on four more years of driving all over Virginia to meet more people to hear their stories and get more perspectives. I was going to run for governor again—and win—in 2013.

I hated losing that 2009 primary, but looking back now I can say that losing was one of the best things that ever happened to me. By then I'd already toured every corner and crossroads of the state, but over the next four years I went to every nook and cranny of Virginia and talked to people about what they needed out of their state government and where they hoped the future would take them—and take Virginia. I had time to soak it all up. I'd always loved history, and if you love U.S. history, it starts with Virginia history. Those four years gave me a deep and living connection to that history—and I saw it pointing to the future.

When you're out listening to people one on one, there's nowhere to hide. It's just you, unfiltered, and you'd better like listening to people. Simple, right? But I think it's a point worth mentioning and remembering. Two of the national politicians I got to know well when I was getting started in politics in the early 1980s were Bill Clinton and Dick Gephardt, and both of them loved that part of it, getting out there and soaking up a real sense of what's important to an individual voter.

I laugh to myself sometimes when I read references to Bill Clinton and how much he loved talking to celebrities. In fairness, he loves to talk to *everybody*. I've seen the man walk through a hotel kitchen and stop and talk to a busboy or dishwasher for half an hour, really listening. He'd have half their life story in no time and he'd find some point of connection. That was a knack of his, a natural gift he had for connecting with people, really understanding where people came from and what they cared about.

I was always that kind of person, going back to when I was knocking on doors as a fourteen-year-old in Syracuse asking people if they wanted my crew to come in and work on their driveway. But the more you talk to people face-to-face, the better a listener you become. I'd ordered a bunch of reporter's notebooks and wherever I went in Virginia, I always had one of those handy. I filled up notebook after notebook with ideas and impressions from people in every corner of the commonwealth. I've still got them, dozens of notebooks filled up from the first page to the last.

Those four extra years helped to reinforce my vision of Virginia's future, which was that this was a state ready to make great progress, with a surge in new jobs to give working people a better quality of life. I visited Jamestown, Virginia, where the first permanent English settlement was founded in 1607. It all started right here in Virginia. We are the cradle of American democracy. We've had a lot of great presidents come from this state, but to me George Washington was our greatest. They wanted to make him king, they wanted to give him that title, and he said no, he didn't want that. He led the fight to found our country and brought it together. What an inspiration. However, we can never forget that for all we admire about him, he was also a slave owner, which, in his writings, he made clear he knew was wrong. The first slaves in North America arrived from Ghana four hundred years ago in Virginia in 1619, twenty of them, at Fort Monroe.

I knew even before I was elected governor in 2013 that racism and its legacies would challenge me in my time in office. I'll admit that a lot of it just confused me. Growing up in upstate New York, I was aware of racism, but never encountered it directly. I was born in February 1957, so through the turmoil of the 1960s, the assassination of Dr. Martin Luther King Jr., and the race riots, I was a St. Ann's elementary school kid more focused on playing football in the mud than on what was going on nationally.

Like too many white Americans, I had much to learn about how deeply entwined racism is in our society. Traveling the country working in national politics beginning in 1979, I saw racism's evil hand in denying African Americans access to voting. During my time as DNC chairman from 2001 to 2005, I launched the Voting Rights Institute to develop practical ideas on how we could protect everyone's right to vote. I appointed former Atlanta Mayor Maynard Jackson and former Jesse Jackson organizer

Donna Brazile to head up the effort, and they continuously updated me on numerous incidents of African Americans being denied their constitutional right to vote.

"Terry was always a leader on diversity, he was always a leader on inclusion," says Minyon Moore, also a former field organizer for Jesse Jackson, whom I hired as CEO of the DNC.

We all knew what the Republicans were up to in the South. They were looking to deny people of color the right to vote by whatever means they could. "The goal of the Democratic Party is to make sure that everybody who has a right to vote in this country can go into those polls and can vote," I told Tim Russert on the NBC program *Meet the Press* in October 2004. "We know what the Republicans are trying to do. They're going to try and disenfranchise voters.

"Now who gets disenfranchised? Predominantly, it's the African American community, which supports this party 92 percent of the time. It's the Hispanic community that votes for this party 66 percent of the time. . . . I have spent four years dealing with these issues, started the Voting Rights Institute to make sure that we are promoting and protecting that right to vote in this country. I want everybody to feel comfortable. When you go vote this time, we're going to make sure that you can go in, you can vote, and we are going to make sure that those votes get counted. There's a big difference between our parties."

The issue of voting rights was one that could bring people together. It was basic and fundamental to restoring faith in our system of government. I remember back in August 2001, early in my time as DNC chair, I flew to San Antonio, Texas, to give a luncheon speech to the National Conference of State Legislatures. My traveling aide that day was Justin. He missed his flight to Texas, came in late, and found a seat at a table in the back.

"People fought and died for the right to vote in this country and I'll be damned if anyone thinks they can take those rights away," I said in my speech that day.

That brought a standing ovation. A young state senator from Illinois sitting next to Justin told him he liked what I'd said and wanted to meet me afterward.

"Chairman, this is Barack Obama," Justin said, introducing us.

Obama told me he was considering a run for U.S. Senate from Illinois and would like my help. He wanted to emphasize social justice and said he loved what I'd said about voting rights. I told him that as national chairman I was precluded from backing one Democrat in a primary, but wanted to hear his ideas and looked forward to following up. A couple of times when I was in Chicago after that, I had lunch with this dynamic, up-and-coming state senator. As we were planning the 2004 Democratic National Convention in Boston, I pushed for Obama to be given the keynote speaking slot, since I knew he was going to electrify the crowd and the nation, as he had been lighting up crowds in Illinois that year running for the US Senate.

I was incredibly proud when Barack Obama was elected president of the United States in November 2008. Of course, as chairman of her campaign, I'd rather have seen Hillary Clinton elected. I was out there front and center on her behalf up until we'd counted all the primary votes and it was time to come together behind our nominee. From that day on I was 100 percent behind Barack Obama. Within days after Hillary's concession speech, she and I hosted several hundred of her top supporters at the Mayflower Hotel in Washington for an event with Senator Obama to unify our party behind his nomination. Senator Obama had run a visionary campaign, and Hillary and I knew he'd make a great president.

Shockingly, having a black man in the White House enflamed bigotry in many parts of the country. I never saw this coming, I'll tell you right now. It's so hard for me to understand. But to these racists, having a black man in the White House was an affront, and the Obama years tragically unleashed an ugly racism that had been smoldering under the surface, as we would come to learn.

Late in my race for governor in 2013, President Obama joined me for a campaign event at a high school in Arlington, Virginia, and gave a rousing speech on my behalf. It was a proud day for me, my family, and the campaign staff, and a fitting way to wrap up the campaign, a strong show of Democratic strength. It was also a lot of fun.

"First of all, I think it's clear that he's not shy," Obama told the crowd, with me standing next to him, breaking into a smile. "This is a man who knows how to work and he knows how to push through obstacles, and he cares deeply about the opportunities that this country has given him, and he wants to make sure that those opportunities are there for everybody—not just for a few. He knows what it's like to work hard and struggle to get ahead."

I was so honored to hear these words from President Obama that day, which may have summed up my time as governor of Virginia better than any of us could have ever known. "I hope you're ready to fight for Terry, because he's ready to fight for you for the next four years," he called out to a burst of applause. "And this election is going to say a lot about Virginia's future and about the country's future."

As governor I had my own little air force, two King Air airplanes and the use of the State Police helicopter fleet. I loved flying on the helicopter. I could get almost anywhere I wanted with it, since it could land at a fire station or in a school soccer field. I loved how low it flew. I was so close to the ground, people would wave to me from their backyards. The view was tremendous, especially during the fall when the leaves had turned. I had a bird's-eye view of our cities, suburbs and towns, farms and waterways, and wide-open fields. It was just spectacular.

I would always bound into the helicopter, pull on my headphones, and have the exact same exchange with my pilot, Lieutenant Jay Cullen.

"How it's look today?" I'd say.

"Great," Jay would say.

"Let me know if you need any help with the controls," I'd tell him.

He'd chuckle and say, "I think I've got it covered, Governor."

One major adjustment of life in the governor's mansion is having your State Police EPU with you all the time. They become part of the family, you're with them so much. They were great with all of our kids, especially our two youngest, Sally and Peter.

"Berke was one of my best friends, especially when I first moved to Richmond," Sally says now. "At the beginning it was really hard because I didn't have a lot of friends in Richmond. I was new. And it was hard to talk to my friends back at home, because I wasn't seeing them every day. I kind of felt isolated for a while. He would make me laugh. He was someone I could share things with. He wouldn't gossip. He would let me tell him whatever and he would give me honest, good advice."

It's funny what kids remember. When Sally met Berke, one of the first things she noticed was his cologne. "You could smell him around the corner," she says. Neither Dorothy nor I remember that. Berke was definitely a character. He was always larger than life.

The first time I met Berke was in late June 2013. Vice President Joe Biden was flying into Richmond to campaign for me, and an hour before the vice president's plane landed I stopped at the Wawa convenience store across from the airport to get a soda. There were eight motorcycle troopers inside with their big leather boots, clearly part of the motorcade there to escort the vice president for the day. I walked over and introduced myself to the troopers.

"You look familiar," Berke said.

"I hope so," I told him. "I'm running for governor, and I've spent a fortune on TV commercials."

He laughed.

"Well, I'm not sure I'm going to vote for you, but I'll make sure you have a safe ride today," he said.

Before we went to Virginia's annual Democratic fund-raiser, we stopped off for a surprise visit at Croaker's Spot, a Richmond soul-food restaurant on Hull Street famous for their fried fish. Biden loves that kind of campaigning, too.

"You know the next governor of Virginia, Terry McAuliffe, right?" he asked, introducing me to people inside. "You're going to vote for my friend here, right?"

We sat down to enjoy the great food at Croaker's, joined by Dorothy and Congressman Bobby Scott of Newport News. On our way out I saw Berke, and he smiled at me. He loved that we'd made the stop at Croaker's.

"I may vote for you after all," he told me that day.

Sally had been in the same school in McLean from kindergarten through eighth grade, and was really nervous about the challenge of starting high school in Richmond, where she had no friends. Her first day came not long after we'd moved and she was just getting to know Berke. He drove her over to school in a big black State Police SUV, and tried to make small talk, but she was having none of it. She was busy being uneasy. As they pulled up to St. Catherine's School, the seniors were all lined up out front to greet new students. Sally was hoping to keep as low a profile as possible.

"Berke put the blue lights and siren on and got on the loud-speaker and said, 'Sally McAuliffe has arrived!'" Sally remembers. "He said it twice. My face was just red. I was so embarrassed getting out of the car, I kind of hid. But people thought it was kind of cool and I got questions all day. It ended up being a good icebreaker. I'll never forget that."

CHAPTER 2

Voting Rights

• • •

One of the questions I thought about the most leading up to my inauguration in January 2014 was a basic one: What more can you do to get people involved? How do you engage them and keep them engaged? How do you give every Virginian the feeling of actively participating in our democracy? One thing I knew for sure was that as a leader you had to start every day with the mind-set that you represented everyone and it was your job to do right by them. That included people who voted for you, people who voted against you, and people who didn't vote at all. That included people who respected you and people who claimed to be your sworn enemy.

When you put together your cabinet, you look for the most qualified people for every job, and you try to think about how they'll work together. One thing you have no time for—if you put the needs of your state first—is grudges or personal differences. For the key post of Virginia Secretary of Public Safety and Homeland Security, I turned to none other than Brian Moran, the man who had spent a good portion of 2009 ripping me every chance he had. Look, I could care less about any of the shots Brian had taken at me when we were battling it out for the Democratic nomination for governor. Brian and I got together at one point just to clear the air. I remember it as an easygoing talk. Brian has a different recollection.

"We settled our differences over a beer or two," he says now. "I had to listen to him give me an earful about my campaign, as if I wasn't already beating myself up about it."

Brian was the man for the job, a smart, capable leader who knew the state well. Abraham Lincoln had assembled a "team of rivals" around him, in the best interests of the nation, and I wanted to do that for Virginia as well. As I said in announcing Brian's appointment in December 2013, "Keeping Virginians safe is the highest priority of state government."

From my first days in office I was especially focused on working to give communities that felt marginalized more of a stake in our society. We've been hit by a vicious cycle in recent decades, the politics of cynicism and personal attack pushing more and more people to give up on the whole spectacle as some kind of dog-and-pony show they could neither understand nor stomach. Well, it's no dog-and-pony show. It's our system of government, and it's our best hope for improving peoples' lives. You can't fight cynicism with more cynicism. You can't battle disillusionment by raising a ruckus and calling people names. To restore faith in government and its institutions, you have to be open-minded and think big, and you have to get it done.

I knew that in 2005, Iowa Governor Tom Vilsack had signed an executive order restoring voting rights to convicted felons who had fully paid their debt to society. I wanted to do the same thing in Virginia, but I knew it wouldn't be easy. I'd been talking about this issue for years with my friend and adviser Levar Stoney, who was my top political aide for my 2013 campaign for governor.

Levar was raised in Yorktown, Virginia, by his father, a janitor, and his grandmother, who cleaned houses. At Tabb High School he was both quarterback of the football team and student body president. At James Madison University he was the first African American man elected president of the student government, campaigning with T-shirts that read: RAISE THE BAR—VOTE FOR LEVAR.

Levar and I spent four years driving around Virginia together day after day, through all ninety-five counties and thirty-eight cities. I had my reporter's notebook with me, always ready to write down a suggestion from a Virginian.

"One time in 2012 we were out in Hampton Roads late on a long day of campaigning," Levar remembers. "An African American woman grabbed me by the shoulder and said, 'Where does Terry McAuliffe stand on restoration of voting rights?'"

Levar told her I was for full restoration of voting rights.

"Even for violent offenders?" she asked.

"Why don't we ask him?" Levar said.

He brought me over.

"Absolutely I'm for full restoration of voting rights for everyone," I told her.

Now, at that stage, I'm not sure we knew just how far we could push to right this historic wrong, but I was determined to go for it. As I used to tell Levar all the time back then, as he drove me all over the state: Why would we go through all that we were going through, driving hundreds of miles a day, eating greasy food meal after meal, if we weren't going to go in and shake things up? We were not doing this to play small ball.

Levar was a young man with a future, that was clear to everybody; he had the energy and the ideas and the follow-through. I named him to my cabinet as Secretary of the Commonwealth, the first African American to have that position and at thirty-four, the youngest to hold that office. He was my point person on restoring voting rights.

In April 2014, we streamlined the process to make it easier for people to apply for restored rights and then in June 2015, we restored voting rights for people who owed outstanding court costs or fees. As Levar put it then, "Wait a minute, these guys owe court fees and they can't vote? And these white-collar guys who owe taxes to different localities can still vote? That's just plain not right."

It was all a legacy of Jim Crow, a variation on the poll tax. I never whitewashed Virginia's sordid history. In June 2015, I used my executive authority to remove the Confederate flag from Virginia license plates. I would give tours of the governor's mansion and make sure to include a visit to the former slave quarters. As you enter the mansion, to this day, there are two staircases going upstairs on either side of the formal front hall—the one on the right, built much narrower, was for the slaves to use.

What was shocking to me, as I revisited Virginia history with a fresh sense of purpose, was the open way that racists in positions of power went about pushing back against voting rights of African Americans in the early twentieth century. They were blatant in their racism.

DISFRANCHISING THE NEGRO read a *New York Times* headline from Richmond, Virginia, in May of 1901 about the Virginia constitutional convention that year. "One of the chief objects in calling this convention was to disfranchise the negro voter," the article said. "Many of the most influential men in the State have indicated a disposition to go slow in the matter of taking away the votes of the negroes." After the convention opened that June, *The Times* reported that the notorious racist Carter Glass declared that he would "rather be expelled from the convention than not carry out" the move to deny African Americans the vote.

Glass "was received with a storm of applause" by the gathering, the *Richmond Times-Dispatch* reported on August 15, 1901. "He spoke with the earnestness, the fire and the vim that have characterized all of his addresses in the Senate and in the Constitutional Convention. . . . When he made the remark that the State Convention of last year in its platform did not enter into any combination with 15,000 negroes to permit them to vote upon the question of their disfranchisement, the greatest demonstration of the day occurred. It was evident that the audience was overwhelmingly in sympathy with the sentiment of the remark." That article quoted Glass himself declaring that the gathering "signalizes a revival of . . . that fundamental pronouncement of the Declaration of Independence which asserts equally among equals." Now that is some twisted rationalizing.

And to think Glass, who would go on to have a long career in Washington, was a Democrat. That's something we can never forget. In the end, Glass and the other racists had their way, making changes to the Virginia Constitution "to eliminate the darkey as a force in Virginia politics," as Glass put it, through poll taxes, literacy tests, and laws to disenfranchise felons.

"Discrimination!" Glass explained that year. "Why, that is precisely what we propose. That, exactly, is what this Convention was elected for—to discriminate to the very extremity of permissible action under the limits of the Federal Constitution, with a view to the elimination of every Negro voter who can be gotten rid of legally."

It's our job now to shine a bright light on that history of overt racism embedded in our institutions. We can highlight the progress we've made overall since then, but not at the expense of working to undo the damage. Soaring rhetoric is great, but I like action. I like to focus on ways to make actual change. So as a candidate for governor in 2013, I'd campaigned on restoring voting rights.

Felons who have done their time and completed probation deserve a second chance. At the time I became governor in 2014, the threshold for a crime to be considered a felony was two hundred dollars. So you could write a bad check for $201 to pay for groceries and lose your voting rights for life, even long after you'd done your time and served your probation. We want everyone to have a stake in their government. We want everyone to know that if they do their part, if they pay back their debt to society, they can be made whole again. We can't continue to uphold a system that is stacked against so many of our people. In forty states, it's automatic for felons who've done their time to regain their voting rights.

Effective action starts with doing your homework. We spent more than a year laying the groundwork for an across-the-board move on voting rights. First we moved drug offenses from violent to nonviolent. We kept looking at ways to get more people back the ability to vote. I remember in February 2015, some buddies from law school visited me at the governor's mansion, John Cohlan, Chris Petersen, and John Boland, and we were brainstorming ideas for restoration along with Levar. That was when it really hit me that it was time to make a splash.

"I'm sick of doing this incrementally," I said, turning to Levar. "Too many lives have been hurt. Get with the lawyers and let's figure out a way I can do it for everyone."

"I'm doing the research," Levar insisted. "It takes a little time."

"Speed it up!" I said.

I wanted to move. Levar reached out to A. E. Dick Howard, the preeminent scholar of constitutional law at the University of Virginia who had once clerked for Justice Hugo Black on the U.S. Supreme Court. Dick was executive director of the commission charged by the state legislature with drafting a new Virginia Constitution in 1972. Levar drove over to see him in Charlottesville. We'd been getting a lot of legal advice, but he was *the* expert. I was so passionate about this. I knew the move I wanted to make would cause quite a stir, and I needed it to be legally airtight.

Professor Howard knew Virginia law better than anyone and what he told Levar was unequivocal: The Virginia Constitution he'd helped redraft gave the governor unconditional power to restore voting rights to convicted felons who had repaid their debt to society by serving their time and fulfilling the terms of their probation.

"Would you be willing to put that in writing, Professor?" Levar asked him.

"Absolutely," Professor Howard said.

I was in a meeting in the conference room adjoining the governor's office in Richmond, and my aide, John Heflin, rushed in and told me Levar was waiting outside and urgently needed to see me.

I stepped out of the meeting and into my private office to find Levar with a big smile on his face. He handed me Dick Howard's letter.

"Dick Howard says you unequivocally have the authority," he told me.

I couldn't believe my eyes reading that document. It was time to celebrate! We walked straight across the street to the governor's mansion, and I poured us each a beer out of the newly installed kegerator that I'd purchased for the mansion. We toasted, and it hit me that all those years of travel, six years on the road, were worth it. With a stroke of my pen, I was going to be able to change the lives of hundreds of thousands of Virginians and give them a second chance as full citizens of their communities. Saint Patrick was shining on me that day.

That was the green light we needed. It really opened the door to do what was right. I tell you, Friday, April 22, 2016 was one of the most exciting days of my life. I walked out onto the steps of the state capitol building in Richmond, Dorothy on one side and Levar on the other. There were hundreds of people gathered in front of us, jammed in as close as they could. Word had spread that a major announcement was coming on voting rights, but no one knew what I was about to do.

Standing near the spot where President Abraham Lincoln had addressed newly freed slaves after Richmond fell in April 1865, I used my authority as governor, as clearly articulated in the Virginia state constitution, to right a historic wrong and restore voting rights to 206,000 convicted felons. When I made the announcement, there was a huge gasp from the crowd. No one could believe it. Then there was pandemonium with raucous applause and tears of joy. People were stunned. This had been a fight for people in Virginia for so long, they couldn't believe they—or their loved ones—were actually getting their rights back.

I told the assembled crowd that Senator Glass had stood at this very capitol in 1902 and announced he was rigging the Virginia Constitution to discriminate against African Americans. I reminded people that Glass had said: "I'm doing it to eliminate the darkey as a force in Virginia politics." Well, 114 years later, there was a new sheriff in town, and that wasn't going to fly anymore.

"Too often in both our distant and recent history, politicians have used their authority to restrict peoples' ability to participate in our democracy," I said at the ceremony that day. "Today we are reversing that disturbing trend and restoring the rights of more than two hundred thousand of our fellow Virginians, who work, raise families, and pay taxes in every corner of our commonwealth."

Some Republicans in Virginia went berserk. They were beside

themselves over what I had just done. They were intent on keeping Virginia in the past, with laws as draconian as those of only three other states in denying felons the vote. It was long past time to do something about that. As I told *The New York Times* that day, "There's no question that we've had a horrible history in voting rights as relates to African Americans—we should remedy it."

The Republican House of Delegates speaker and senate majority leader immediately filed a petition in the Virginia Supreme Court challenging my executive order. They asserted that I didn't have the legal authority to make that move. There was no question in my mind that the Supreme Court was going to rule in my favor. I was assured by Attorney General Mark Herring and by A. E. Dick Howard that this was not even a close call.

"The governor's authority to act as he did derives directly from the text of the constitution of Virginia," Howard explained. "The first paragraph of Article V, Section 12, states: 'The Governor shall have power to remit fines and penalties under such rules and regulations as may be prescribed by law; to grant reprieves and pardons after conviction except when the prosecution has been carried on by the House of Delegates; to remove disabilities consequent upon conviction for offenses committed prior or subsequent to the adoption of this Constitution; and to commute capital punishment.' Nowhere—neither in this section nor elsewhere—does the constitution limit the governor to acting in individual cases. The governor's clemency powers are plenary and discretionary. The only limits to his authority are those spelled out in the constitution itself."

Three months later, to my surprise, the Supreme Court ruled against me, 4–3. Virginia is one of two states where the legislature appoints the state Supreme Court. I was shocked when I saw the rationale behind the ruling and saw how constitutionally thin it was.

Now, let's be clear, I'm a member of the District of Columbia and the United States Supreme Court Bar, but my legal career peaked when I argued my only case before a Dewey Beach, Delaware, magistrate at two in the morning a long time ago. I had been a full-time student at Georgetown Law while at the same time running three companies. Luckily, Georgetown did not take attendance. However, I absorbed enough of the law to assume that if the Virginia Supreme Court was going to oppose my order, they ought to base it on constitutional grounds. They didn't.

The law was on my side, as A. E. Dick Howard and my attorney general and all the other experts I'd consulted told me. The argument against righting this historic wrong boiled down to: No governor has done it before, so we won't let McAuliffe do it now.

How's that for an argument? You think I'm making that up? No one could make this stuff up.

"Never before have any of the prior seventy-one Virginia governors issued a clemency order of any kind . . . to a class of unnamed felons without regard for the nature of the crimes or any other individual circumstances relevant to the request," the chief justice, Don Lemons, wrote in a majority opinion.

Never before? That's an argument? The whole point was: If you'd served your time, and served your probation, then you should be welcomed back into society.

I was blistering in my reply to the court's transparent obstructionism. I'd worked hard as governor to bring Virginia into the twenty-first century, a welcoming state that respected the rights of all, a dynamic and future-oriented Silicon Valley of the East where companies could relocate knowing that people of all backgrounds would feel included.

"Once again, the Virginia Supreme Court has placed Virginia as an outlier in the struggle for civil and human rights," I said in a statement. "It is a disgrace that the Republican leadership of Virginia would file a lawsuit to deny more than 200,000 of their own citizens the right to vote. And I cannot accept that this overtly political action could succeed."

I was far from alone in blasting the Virginia Supreme Court.

VIRGINIA'S VOTING RIGHTS DEBACLE was the headline on the *Washington Post* editorial.

"The Virginia Supreme Court ruling that Gov. Terry McAuliffe (D) overstepped his powers in restoring voting rights to 206,000 felons who have completed their sentences is a model of pretzel-twisted reasoning that glosses over the plain language of the state's constitution and elides recent state history to arrive at a conclusion whose effects are as heedless of national trends as they are racially retrograde," the editorial board wrote, adding that the court "failed to cite any constitutional language that would contravene Mr. McAuliffe's power to issue his directive."

A. E. Dick Howard summed it up nicely. "Simply because a constitutional authority has not been exercised previously does not mean it doesn't exist," he told me. "I think the Supreme Court of Virginia simply didn't like what you were doing. That's a policy judgment, that's not a constitutional argument."

Here was the thing, though: The practical result of the ruling was that I couldn't sign one executive order to restore the voting rights of all those who deserved their voting rights restored at one time. I had to restore each individual's rights one by one. Did they think that was going to deter me? If so, they didn't know me. I wasted no time in announcing I'd sign them all one by one, if that was what it took. As that *Washington Post* editorial noted, "Mr. McAuliffe is correct that he is now within his rights to sign—using banks of mechanical autopens—'individual' letters restoring voting rights to the same ex-convicts whose rights are now in jeopardy owing to the court."

As soon as I got the order, I informed my staff I would sign them individually outside by the Civil Rights Memorial on Capitol Square in front of the governor's mansion facing the capitol building. Former Governor Mark Warner and his wife, Lisa, had been instrumental in establishing and funding the memorial, which highlights the courageous efforts by Barbara Johns, leading her classmates out of Moton School in Farmville in 1951, and Oliver Hill and the other lawyers who later worked on the landmark school-desegregation case *Brown v. Board of Education.*

"Let's get out all 206,000 petitions and bring boxes of pens, and I'm going to sit there and sign every damn one, even if takes me a week," I told my new secretary of the commonwealth, Kelly Thomasson.

As soon as I announced the action I was taking, the senate leader and the speaker sued me again, this time for contempt of court. I was honored to be the first Virginia governor sued for contempt of court. I loved it! I had justice on my side, and knew it. This wasn't a game for me. I was fighting more than a century of horrible disenfranchisement. Sure enough, the Virginia Supreme Court, which was being resoundingly criticized around the country for its opinion, quickly tossed out the ridiculous contempt of court motion.

I took the high road in my response. "It is my hope that the court's validation of the process we are using will convince Republicans to drop their divisive efforts to prevent Virginians from regaining their voting rights and focus their energy and resources on making Virginia a better place to live for the people who elected all of us to lead," I said.

It was almost funny. These Republican reactionaries were on the wrong side of history. They couldn't stop us, and in fighting us all they did was help us get the word out. Most of these disenfranchised felons weren't reading newspapers. Many of them didn't even know I'd given them back their voting rights. So when we were forced to make the move on a case-by-case basis, I decided to send out individual letters to every single one of them—which, we soon realized, was a great opportunity.

We ended up sending out 206,000 envelopes containing a beautiful parchment document with the commonwealth seal and my signature, restoring their voting rights. And while I was at it, I included a voter registration form and a self-addressed, stamped envelope. Therefore, I'd like to thank the Republican leadership for allowing me to have one of the largest voter-registration drives in history!

I was able to restore more voting rights than any governor in U.S. history. That was my proudest accomplishment as governor. It was life-changing for so many people. Stories immediately came in from all over the commonwealth of grown men breaking into tears, mothers hugging their children, and widespread jubilation. So many Americans take the right to vote for granted, and too often don't even bother to vote, and for these men and women this brought redemption. I've had fathers come up to me and tell me about how ashamed they were that they couldn't vote. They'd go to a polling station on election day to try to find one of those "I voted" stickers someone had tossed aside, so they could put that on before they went home. They were embarrassed to tell their kids they couldn't vote.

So many men and women came up to me later to thank me. They felt their lives, or the lives of those close to them, had meaning again because of getting their voting rights back. Not only did these people have their voting rights restored, they also were eligible to run for public office, if they chose.

Louise Meckstroth wrote to me about her daughter, Carol Meckstroth Davidson, who served her time and was released. "I wondered how long it would take for her to get over the fact that she was now a felon," Louise wrote to me about her daughter in March 2017. "She has worked hard, done all the right things as to addressing her addictions and attitudes, is an active member of Alcoholics Anonymous and frequently also serves as a mentor for those who need some extra help. . . . The only thing I have heard her mention is that she hoped someday to be able to vote, maybe even run for local office and travel out of the country if she wishes to—and now she can do those things that the rest of us take for granted. . . . I cannot thank you enough for recognizing Carol's commitment and the way she lives her life—it could not have come at a better time for her!"

I remember one man in particular, Haywood Barnes, a retired crane operator who had worked at the Norfolk Naval Shipyard for thirty-two years, who had been convicted of a felony at a young age. I went down to Portsmouth to personally give him his certificate. He was sick, so I had to give it to his daughter, Rose Davis, to present to him. He was going to vote for the first time in his life after more than sixty years of hoping for that honor. It was going to be the greatest thing that ever happened for him, but unfortunately, he died just before election day. We thought that was sad, but his daughter called and gave me a different perspective.

"Governor, when I gave him the certificate he smiled for the first time in a long, long time," she told me. "He was looking forward to voting in the election, but don't be sad. He died with a smile on his face because you made him a full citizen of the commonwealth of Virginia."

CHAPTER 3

A New President

■ ■ ■

O ne thing I never got from Hillary Clinton or any of her key advisers in the weeks leading up to the November 2016 presidential election was complacency. Yes, she had cleaned Donald Trump's clock in all three televised presidential debates. She stood up there in front of the American people and called Donald Trump a "puppet" of Vladimir Putin to his face. Boy, did she hit the nail on the head! Yes, she had a lead in the polls as election day neared. And yes, we knew more Americans would be voting for her than for Trump. All true. But none of us could ever forget that the road to the White House ended with the electoral college, not the popular vote. We remembered December 2000, when Vice President Al Gore was denied the presidency by the U.S. Supreme Court ordering a halt in the recounting of Florida votes. You take nothing for granted if you're in politics.

Donald Trump, as most of us knew, was dangerous. I never got the appeal of *The Apprentice*. Trump was overrated as a businessman with a string of bankruptcies behind him, despite having a rich dad who set him up with more than $413 million; in today's dollars, almost half a billion. Trump was famous in New York for always stiffing the little guy and never paying his bills. The whole setup of the show was that he was some kind of dynamo business-man, which was a joke, but he played the part and people ate it up.

Trump ran for president like he was filming another season of *The Apprentice*, and it worked. He tossed out his stupid little nicknames. He bluffed and bullied his way through it all, and almost started to convince himself he knew what he was talking about even when he was making things up left and right. He was somehow the last one standing after more than a dozen Repub-lican candidates exhausted themselves trading insults and beating each other up. Trump was going to do whatever it took to win. In 1999 he proclaimed, "I am very pro-choice," and then somehow became a big pro-lifer when he went after the votes of evangeli-cals. Trump was a Democrat for most of his life and then pre-tended to be a Republican to win the nomination for president. If he'd thought he could have won the Democratic nomination, he'd have run as a Democrat, but the field was too competitive on that side, so instead he pretended he was a Republican. He wasn't a Republican. He was a Trump.

I remember once in February 2001, just after Bill Clinton left the White House, President Clinton and I spent a night visiting my good friends Howard and Michele Kessler at their home in Florida. I was DNC chair at the time and had to get up for an early-morning appearance on CNN. I got about two hours of sleep, and then President Clinton and I went over to meet Trump at his golf course.

We were standing around on the first tee, a 475-yard par four, staring down the fairway, when Trump brought out a big choco-late birthday cake. It was my forty-fourth birthday and everyone sang "Happy Birthday" to me. One thing struck me as odd. We were in the pro shop after our round and Trump had left for about ten minutes. He came back with a big manila envelope full of pictures of us out on the golf course, which he gave to President Clinton. OK, that was nice. Then we noticed Trump had signed them, "To Bill, best wishes, Donald." First of all, how about a "Mr. President"? The man had just left the White House with the highest approval rating of any two-term president since they started keeping records. Beyond that, I remember thinking, "What in the heck is Bill Clinton going to do with a pile of autographed pictures of Donald Trump?"

Trump came down to Virginia in August 2014 for an event for the Jimmy Valvano Foundation, named in honor of the famous basketball coach, to raise money to fight cancer. Trump and I both flew in to the event by helicopter. My State Police helicopter landed first and when Trump arrived, he was very jacked up to tell me that his helicopter was much bigger than mine, which it was. He couldn't stop talking about it.

Trump's vineyard in Virginia was hosting the event and we did a tour of the winery.

"This is the best governor in America!" Trump told the audience that night.

Trump had always been a Democrat going way back, and had written checks to a lot of Democrats. He donated $25,000 to my 2009 campaign for Virginia governor, and I'd expected him to donate again when I ran in 2013. I went up to New York with Patrick Hallahan and Jay Dunn of my finance team to see Trump in his office, which is a shrine to himself. He told me he couldn't write me another check, not then anyway.

"No, I'm thinking maybe I'll run for president," he said. "This may not help me if I decide to run as a Republican."

That took me aback.

"Wouldn't you run as a Democrat?" I asked him.

"I'm not sure," he said.

Trump had been threatening for years to run for president. No one ever knew how seriously to take him. Back in December 1999 he published an article in *The Wall Street Journal* saying he was seriously considering running. Not as a Democrat or a Republican, but with something called the Reform Party. His inspiration? The former professional wrestler Jesse "The Body" Ventura, who at the time was governor of Minnesota. "Ventura has strongly encouraged me to seek the nomination, and I highly respect Jesse as the embodiment of the political qualities America needs and voters reward."

Donald Trump was the first reality TV star to run for president on a major-party ticket and he milked it for everything it was worth. Like most of the country, I was shocked when he was elected president and beyond disappointed. Hillary Clinton would have been a great president. But as governor, I had a job to do and that job was putting the people of my state first.

It was my job as governor to get along with the new president and to give him the benefit of the doubt. I wanted to work with him where I could. Virginia is home to nearly thirty military bases, including the largest naval base in the world, Naval Station Norfolk. The Pentagon is in Arlington, Virginia. CIA headquarters is in Langley, Virginia. Quantico, Virginia, houses the FBI academy and a large Marine Corps base. I could go on and on. We couldn't afford to take a hit on defense-industry jobs the way we had during sequestration. In fact, we wanted more government spending in Virginia. Like governors across the country, I wanted Trump to make a priority of passing a major infrastructure bill, an initiative we all knew was long overdue.

Five weeks after the inauguration, I went to the White House for the annual governors dinner, the first major social event of the administration, joined by my daughter Mary. I'd been elected vice chair of the National Governors Association in December 2014, and took over as NGA chair in July 2016, so I was seated next to Trump at the black tie event.

My whole mind-set was to try to find common ground with the new president. He was friendly that night in January 2017. At one point he leaned over and grabbed my arm for emphasis.

"Terry, can you believe I'm here?" he said.

"No disrespect, Mr. President, but no, sir," I told him, smiling.

He couldn't believe it either. He was as surprised as the rest of us to find himself sitting in the White House as president of the United States, and it was obvious that he was going to make it up as he went along.

A month earlier, just after the inauguration, President Trump had wasted no time using the power of his office to demonize foreigners. On Friday, January 27, he'd issued an executive order seeking to block citizens from Iran, Iraq, Syria, Yemen, Sudan, Libya, and Somalia from entering the United States for the next ninety days without "extreme vetting," a move that produced instant fear, chaos, and consternation. No one knew what it meant, least of all the authorities who had to enforce it.

The next morning, I was tipped off that some U.S. citizens arriving at Dulles International Airport in Virginia were being held in detention for hours without access to legal representation. I knew I had to get up to Dulles to raise holy hell. I was outraged. I called Attorney General Herring, and asked him to meet me at Dulles for a 2 p.m. press conference.

It was mayhem up there. There were hundreds of activists chanting, "No hate! No fear! Refugees are welcome here!" and holding up signs. I couldn't believe U.S. citizens were being held for hours despite doing nothing wrong, just because they happened to be flying in from one of the countries on the list in the Trump executive order. I was particularly concerned about one Virginia family with two children that had been held for hours. This was the United States of America! These children were U.S. citizens. You can't do that to people! I was irate, and it showed when I talked to reporters and called on the president to reverse his ban on refugees.

"People have boarded planes, allowed to come to this country, and when they land in our country, they're detained," I said. "What kind of nation is this? We were built on immigrants, they have made our country the great nation it is today, and it is sending such a discriminatory, racist message. It is awful, it's got to stop."

I announced I wasn't leaving the airport until these Virginians held in detention were given access to legal representation. Listen, we all want to keep our country safe, but this had nothing to do with that. This was all about Donald Trump peddling hate, inflaming the emotions of what he considered his base. He was pushing hatred as he would again and again and again throughout his time in office.

On February 8, we got word that a dozen ICE agents had surrounded a group of Latino men just after they had come out of the Rising Hope United Methodist Mission Church in Alexandria, Virginia, and taken them into custody with no probable cause. A church is supposed to be a sanctuary. I was infuriated and wanted answers. I sent a letter to Secretary of Homeland Security John Kelly asking if ICE agents were targeting places of worship to detain people. If so, that would clearly be improper. I asked the secretary to explain the criteria ICE agents were relying on to decide when and where and how to detain people for questioning.

I was furious about what the Trump administration was

doing because it wasn't legal, and also because of the havoc it was wreaking on the people of Virginia. So many small businesses in Northern Virginia were owned by foreign-born individuals. Many of these immigrants were scared to death. They thought they were going to get arrested and deported. That could have a crippling impact on our state economy. I did a tour of small businesses to find out what was going on and found out just how wide an impact this was having.

As *The Washington Post* reported, "McAuliffe has written to the Trump administration about the issue and made a point of touting the state's diversity as an economic asset. On Wednesday, he toured the Fair Price International Supermarket in the Alexandria area of Fairfax County and praised the initiative shown by immigrants. Market owner Saqib Choubhry, who arrived in the United States fourteen years ago from Pakistan, told the governor that 'people are scared' since the presidential election, and that his Middle Eastern customers come less often and buy fewer goods."

Choubhry was preparing to expand his business and open new stores, but in that environment he put all his expansion plans on hold, costing Virginia jobs.

I needed to get a reliable answer on just what U.S. policy was. Who was being arrested? When could they be released? What was the actual policy? No one seemed to know for sure. So I had my scheduler, Yael Belkind, set up a private meeting with Secretary Kelly during the first NGA meeting of Trump's presidency, along with Paul Reagan, my chief of staff, Brian Moran, secretary of public safety, and Maribel Ramos, who ran Virginia's Washington office.

"Mr. Secretary, on behalf of the governors, we need to know: What is the Trump policy on immigration?" I asked when we met that Sunday. "I've got an international airport in my state, as do many governors, and our folks are terrified."

I emphasized that the chaos was creating a huge problem in Northern Virginia, where so many immigrants had small businesses and were terrified that they were about to be deported. This was how Secretary Kelly summed up, according to notes taken by Maribel at the time.

"Let me be clear, Governor, the policy of the Trump administration is that no illegal alien will be deported unless they commit a serious criminal offense," he said.

"So you're telling me, Mr. Secretary, I can go back and tell the governors, and tell Virginians, and tell the press that undocumented immigrants are safe?" I followed up. "The only undocumented immigrants who are not going to be safe are those who commit a serious criminal offense?"

"That is the policy," he said.

"I think the vast majority of Americans would agree with that policy statement, Mr. Secretary," I told him.

So I went out and briefed the press and the governors-only meeting on the policy. John Kelly is a four-star Marine general. I have nothing but respect for the Marines. Of course I believed him when he told me that.

However, not long after that meeting, ICE detained a Virginia resident during a routine check-in for an outstanding infraction she had for driving with a broken headlight. Liliana Cruz Mendez, a mother of two, had come to this country from El Salvador, and now ICE wanted to deport her for a broken headlight! There were heartbreaking pictures of her in the papers with her two children and husband before they were separated and she was taken away in a white ICE van.

A broken headlight is not a serious crime. I did what I could as governor to help her. I pardoned her and took away the underlying offense. "While this pardon will not necessarily ensure that U.S. Immigration and Customs Enforcement agrees to return Ms.

Mendez to her husband and two children, I hope it will send a clear message that tearing this family apart will not make our commonwealth or our country safer," I said at the time.

A month later, they deported her anyway, leaving behind her two children, who were both U.S. citizens. It was a travesty. What had happened since I'd spoken to Secretary Kelly? The problem was, he had to deal with a totally dysfunctional White House that was not being honest with him, and an influx of thousands of new ICE agents who were not always easy to monitor or control. For Kelly it was a nightmare. Later, after he'd left the administration, he echoed my point that these people just didn't know what they were doing, or as he put it, "They got a little bit maybe out in front of their skis."

My other big beef with Trump that year was health care. Trump had run against one of the signature achievements of the Obama administration, the Affordable Care Act, campaigning on a policy of "repeal and replace." His first day in office, he issued an executive order that sought to undermine the ACA and he took shots at it whenever he could. The problem was, as with so many other issues, he didn't seem to have much of an idea what he was talking about once the discussion moved past slogans. Everybody had been telling him for months that this was a very complex, difficult issue and he never listened.

When he spoke to the National Governors Association soon after he became president, he actually told us, "Now I have to tell you, it's an unbelievably complex subject. Nobody knew that health care could be so complicated."

Are you kidding me? We all knew. The whole nation had been grappling with the complexities of health care for decades, and on the campaign trail Trump tried to come off as the expert of all experts. He was going to simplify it for us all. Now he was saying this to a room full of governors who had all administered complex health-care programs in their states? We'd all been trying to get through to him how complex this was. The governors just looked at each other and shook their heads in bewilderment over that one.

That July, President Trump came to Norfolk, Virginia, for the commissioning ceremony for the USS *Gerald R. Ford,* the world's largest aircraft carrier. I was there for the occasion along with many Ford administration notables, including former Vice President Dick Cheney and former Defense Secretary Don Rumsfeld. Trump and I sat next to each other on the dais. I had the president sitting next to me for an hour. I wasn't going to miss the opportunity to speak up. He was creating chaos in our health-care delivery system and we were already feeling the impact of that.

"Mr. President, you ran on fixing health care," I told him. "You said more people would get access, it would be better care, and it would be cheaper. You ran on that, but you're doing the opposite."

"You're right," he said. "I'm not making any progress with the Republicans. I need to do it. I think I can do a deal with the Democrats on this."

"Good, let's get it going," I said.

"Why don't you come up and have lunch with me on Wednesday at the White House?" he said. "We've got a great chef. And we'll talk about it."

"Great," I said.

What else do you tell the president of the United States when he says he wants to have lunch and make a deal? That was Saturday. I called up the Democratic leadership in Congress to brief them. I said I had no idea if Trump was serious about wanting to make a deal with Democrats, but it seemed worth following up. I was going to call back before Wednesday to confirm the meeting, but before I could do that Trump blew the whole thing up.

He took to Twitter on Tuesday morning for one of his typical early-morning rants, rambling on about how it was a "Big day for HealthCare. After 7 years of talking, we will soon see whether or not Republicans are willing to step up to the plate!" Then another one: "ObamaCare is torturing the American People. The Democrats have fooled the people long enough. Repeal or Repeal & Replace! I have pen in hand." And: "It is time to end the Obamacare Nightmare!"

He also announced he was heading to Ohio that night for one of his bizarre rallies to stir up his core supporters. It was clear he'd rather attack Democrats wildly on health care than make a deal and get something done. No way was I going up to the White House to have lunch with him that week. Once again, Donald Trump had chosen to veer back toward pitting one side against the other, building up resentment rather than looking for a way to bring people together and to make progress.

CHAPTER 4

The Robert E. Lee Statue

...

We knew early in 2017 that we might have a problem on our hands in Charlottesville. It started on February 6, 2017, when the Charlottesville City Council voted to remove a statue of General Robert E. Lee from its spot in the middle of Lee Park not far from the University of Virginia. The Charlottesville Circuit Court later blocked any action to remove or sell the statue, delaying action for six months, but that didn't stop white nationalists from using the planned move as a rallying cry.

The whole issue of Confederate ideology had been percolating in the South for generations, but it was thrust into the forefront in June 2015 when a twenty-one-year-old white supremacist murdered nine African Americans at the Emanuel African Methodist Episcopal Church in Charleston, South Carolina, including Clementa Pinckney, a pastor and state senator. All the publicity about the terrorist and his incoherent ranting put the spotlight on a virulent new mix of neo-Nazism, white supremacy, and identification with the Confederate cause.

Seventy-seven percent of the jurisdictions in Virginia have a

Confederate monument. The Revolutionary War is such an important part of our history, from Patrick Henry's famous "Give me liberty or give me death" speech in March 1775 at St. John's Church in Richmond to the final battle at Yorktown. Of the 429 war memorials in Virginia, only four are for the Revolutionary War. Four! There are twenty-seven for the Union cause in the Civil War. The Second World War, the war that defeated Hitler and his Third Reich? Seven monuments. World War I, the Great War, the "war to end all wars," merits only six monuments. And the Confederacy? There are 378 Confederate monuments across Virginia, most of which were built during the Jim Crow era when laws were enacted across the South to enforce racial segregation.

The Lee statue in Charlottesville was not erected in the years soon after the Confederacy was defeated in the Civil War in 1865, with Lee surrendering to General Ulysses S. Grant at Appomattox. In Virginia, only twenty were built from 1869 to 1879. From 1900 to 1909, ninety were built. From 1910 to 1919, over sixty were built. From 1920 to 1929, fifty-five were built, including the statue at Lee Park.

Like most of these monuments erected all over the South, the Lee statue very much had a political message to impart. It was donated by the segregationist Paul Goodloe McIntire in 1924, the same year Virginia passed a Racial Integrity Act to prohibit interracial marriages. That tells you something about the context.

The statue "embodied the Lost Cause interpretation of the Civil War, which romanticized the Confederate past and suppressed the horrors of slavery and slavery's role as the fundamental cause of the war while affirming the enduring role of white supremacy," a Blue Ribbon Commission on race, memorials, and public spaces empaneled by the Charlottesville City Council put in a report released in December 2016.

Robert E. Lee's great-granddaughter spoke at the dedication of the statue in May 1924, remembering her ancestor as a man who she said represented "the moral greatness of the Old South." For her, the Civil War was not about slavery, it was about differing "interpretations of our Constitution" and differing "ideals of democracy." She was wrong. It was about slavery and it was about treason, pure and simple, and we know the deep and lasting damage that comes with running away from that central truth. As President Abraham Lincoln made clear before the war in his "House Divided" speech in June 1858, it would be a war about whether the country could remain "half slave and half free."

The Charlottesville City Council knew that its vote to remove the statue was sure to rile up the various segments of the alt-right, white supremacists, neo-Nazis, and other racists, but what made everything worse was that all over the country those groups had already been riled up. At the end of January, the mayor held a press conference to declare Charlottesville a "capital of resistance" to newly inaugurated President Trump and his anti-immigrant agenda.

That afternoon, Brian Moran came into my office to tell me face-to-face.

"Governor, I have some bad news," he said. "We're going to have a problem. I'm worried they're trying to turn Charlottesville into Berkeley. They've declared it the capital of the resistance."

"Are you (expletive) kidding me?" I said, exasperated, then immediately turned to practical considerations.

"Get your folks together and figure out what we need to do," I said.

Understand, I ran for governor of Virginia on a platform of bringing the commonwealth into the twenty-first century. What did that mean? Mostly it boiled down to two related priorities—one was making Virginia a welcoming and tolerant state where people wanted to live, and the other was finding smart ways to bring in investment to supercharge the economy and generate good-paying jobs that could help people achieve a better quality of life. Our efforts were paying off. I'd brought in a record infusion of new investment to spur job growth, nearly $20 billion of new capital from around the globe. We'd made Virginia the leader in cyber security, data centers and data analytics, unmanned systems, and the list went on and on. We had dropped unemployment from 5.4 percent down to 3.6 percent.

In February 2017 came the news that I had successfully recruited Nestlé Corporation, the world's largest food and beverage company, to move its U.S. headquarters from Southern California to Arlington, Virginia, bringing in 750 high-paying jobs. "For northern Virginia, the arrival of Nestle USA which in 2015 had $9.7 billion in sales, serves as proof that it can look beyond defense contractors for growth," *The Washington Post* reported. "The state is now home to more than seventy corporate headquarters, including Volkswagen Group of America, Hilton Worldwide and Capitol One Financial." A year later came the announcement that Amazon was choosing Northern Virginia as one of its two new major headquarters, bringing in a minimum of twenty-five thousand jobs. We could never have made all that progress—"jobs, jobs, jobs"—if we hadn't fought to make Virginia a more appealing place to live.

Over my four years as governor, I vetoed a record 120 bills passed by the Republican legislature that would alienate people: gun bills that did not make our communities safer; bills that would have hurt our environment; or bills that would have rolled back voting rights. In 2013, before I was elected, the Republican legislature passed—and a Republican governor signed—an outrageous bill called the transvaginal bill, which would have required any woman considering an abortion to undergo a horribly invasive procedure called a "transvaginal ultrasound." The more you heard about it the more outrageous it sounded.

As *The Economist* wrote, "Making this invasive procedure, involving the insertion of a wand, compulsory is akin, say Democrats and women's rights advocates, to a sexual assault. The aim, supposedly, is to confront women with the reality of their fetus."

I can't tell you how many times I turned on the TV and heard our state being mocked after the transvaginal bill was signed into law in March 2012. Rachel Maddow on MSNBC and Jon Stewart on *The Daily Show* had a field day with this. It was embarrassing for Virginia.

Most innovative technology companies don't want to move to a state that discriminates against women and where they are shutting down Planned Parenthood clinics and other women's health centers. These clinics offer a variety of services—testing and treatment of sexually transmitted diseases primarily (41 percent of Planned Parenthood visits), contraception (34 percent), and cancer screening (10 percent). Abortions accounted for just 3 percent of Planned Parenthood services annually, according to the group's statistics. The Republicans in the state legislature wanted to defund all women's health clinics, with no alternative in mind for the tens of thousands of women who depended on these clinics for health care. I vetoed that one as well.

We'd worked hard from day one to send the message that our state was open to everyone. The last thing we wanted was for people to think Virginia was for haters. That was the message that could be delivered by a bunch of people coming into our state carrying torches and chanting horrible, racist slurs. That puts up a "not wanted" sign for businesses. Everything we had worked to build for three years was in jeopardy.

The question we were always asking was: How are we going to encourage these big new innovative technology companies to relocate to Virginia? We'd spent a record amount of money on education and other state programs to improve quality of life, but we also had to show that we were open and welcoming.

I ran for governor against a right-wing candidate, Ken Cuccinelli, who believed more in demonizing people than in bringing people together. That might play to a fringe element, but it's not what Virginia is about—and it's not going to help you bring investment to your state. That won't work if you're anti-woman, anti-gay, anti-tolerance.

"It's difficult to grow an economy when you call gay Virginians 'soulless and self-destructive' human beings," I said at my first debate with Cuccinelli at the Homestead hotel in Hot Springs, Virginia.

A few minutes later, I talked about why so many Republican business leaders in Virginia had endorsed me, knowing what I could do for the state. I told a story about Cuccinelli and I recently speaking to the Northern Virginia Technology Council.

"We both spoke," I said. "He said to this leading group of business leaders, 'I haven't been extreme on social issues,' and you know what happened? They laughed at him."

Cuccinelli was stunned. He had nothing to say. Silence dragged out for several seconds. It was awkward that the man had no defense. Finally, moderator Judy Woodruff spoke up and asked in a hushed tone, "Mr. Cuccinelli, do you want to respond?"

"Yeah, you know, four people in the front thought that was all real funny," he said, his voice unsteady.

"I don't think it's funny," I said firmly. "I think it's serious."

The Charlottesville City Council decision on the Robert E. Lee statue in a 3–2 vote did not generate much immediate press attention. There was little newspaper coverage at first beyond a short item that Wednesday in the Staunton, Virginia, *News Leader* on the vote, noting that city staff would have two months "to recommend how to move the imposing equestrian monument," and also that the council voted to change the name of Lee Park, which was renamed Emancipation Park.

"Councilor Wes Bellamy said community members feel the statue is culturally offensive and a symbol of white supremacy," the paper reported. "Councilor Bob Fenwick provided the swing vote after both praising Lee and saying his record of fighting to preserve slavery is undeniable. Mayor Mike Singer [sic] and Councilor Kathy Galvin voted against the resolution, expressing discomfort with the potential cost of moving the statue and of defending the city against legal challenges."

Only a few short notices on the decision had appeared in a small number of newspapers around the country until the following weekend when a former resident of Minnesota named Corey Stewart, an elected official in Prince William County, Virginia, showed up at the Robert E. Lee statue to make some noise. Mostly, Stewart wanted to boost his longshot candidacy for the Republican nomination to succeed me as governor of Virginia. Nothing like a little street theater to generate some headlines. Stewart and his small knot of demonstrators were met by dozens of protesters with signs reading BAN BIGOTS and NO TOLERANCE FOR WHITE SUPREMACY.

"It was the harshest reception yet for the provocative chairman of the Prince William County Board of County Supervisors, who is campaigning for the GOP nomination for governor as Virginia's Donald Trump, with a hard-line stance against illegal immigration," reported Fenit Nirappil in *The Washington Post*.

I knew Stewart. I'd had him to the governor's mansion, like a lot of local elected officials, and in those meetings he'd come across as low-key and reasonable despite his ugly anti-imigrant record. But to give you an idea, this was a man who had been ousted from his position as Virginia chair of Trump's presidential campaign for being too radical. For him, and for other extremists, the vote to remove the statue played right into their hands. This was a great way to fire up their base. Did they care at all about the Robert E. Lee statue? It didn't matter. They just needed a pretext to inflame their fellow extremists. They wanted to ride this as far as they could.

That was especially true of Jason Kessler, a University of Virginia graduate who at that time still lived in Charlottesville. Kessler was an odd duck. He had actually voted for Obama in 2008 and was part of the Occupy Wall Street encampment at UVA in 2011, but he went all in on the "alt-right," a term popularized by another UVA graduate, Richard Spencer, who had been energized by Trump's election and saw it as encouragement to extremists. Spencer was known to lead his followers in chants of "Heil Trump!" and "Let's party like it's 1933." The guy loved Hitler. They were looking for excuses to come out of the shadows, to leave their basements and closets, and the move to take down the Robert E. Lee statue had given them that excuse.

Kessler and Spencer and a few of their followers showed up at the Robert E. Lee statue on Saturday night, May 13, for a torchlight protest against any move to pull down the statue. It wasn't much. They had thirty or forty knuckleheads with torches, chanting Nazi slogans like "Blood and soil," or "Blut und Boden," as Hitler himself used to put it. They also chanted "You will not replace us," and—this one is strange—"Russia is our friend."

"After about ten minutes, Charlottesville police arrived at the scene following an altercation between protesters," the Charlottesville *Daily Progress* reported. "The crowd quickly dispersed with no further incidents, according to police."

Spencer posted a picture of himself on Twitter that night holding a torch at the rally along with the hashtag #torchlight. Kessler was more enthusiastic, throwing up pictures from the rally on Twitter and calling it a "massive" march to #SaveLeeandJackson. But the next day he posted a video online insisting the rally had more in common with a Viking rally than a KKK rally, characterizing the protesters as being concerned about "white identity. . . . That is their cause. . . . It is time to stop apologizing. It is time to stop running away."

Kessler meant those words more literally than anyone could have known at the time. He had plans. He was clearly delusional, but he was also ambitious. He thought this was his moment, even if to most of the rest of the world his actions looked tired and predictable, an old act.

As Vinson Cunningham later wrote in *The New Yorker,* in an article headlined THE UGLY, VIOLENT CLICHÉS OF WHITE-SUPREMACIST TERRORISM, "A friend of mine, who's black, was in Charlottesville in May, and, walking home, ran into Spencer's protest. He was frozen by the torchlight, awed, almost, by the pagan intensity of the crowd's idol worship, and had to shake himself out of a daze before he ran. He soon skipped town for a while—he'd been there for months, on a fellowship—the whole time dreading going back. Unsurprising, sure, all of it, but terror all the same."

Two and a half weeks after the Saturday night torch-lit march in May, Kessler filed paperwork with the City of Charlottesville Parks & Recreation Department, applying for a permit for a "Unite the Right" rally at the Robert E. Lee statue on Saturday, August 12. When asked for a description of the event, he wrote out in block letters, "FREE SPEECH RALLY IN SUPPORT OF THE LEE MONUMENT." Kessler's scheme was to pull white nationalists, neo-Nazis, and other right-wing extremists from all over the country to converge on Charlottesville in broad daylight.

CHAPTER 5

Preparing for Trouble

• • •

I hate to say it, but the City of Charlottesville did itself no favors that June, as we found out later. Their permitting process was pathetic. The city had a rule that said if someone submitted a permit and no action had been taken to approve or reject that permit within ten business days, then it would automatically be approved. Well, can you believe it? No action was taken by the city within the mandatory ten days on Kessler's permit to host a "Unite the Right" rally in Charlottesville that August 12. No attempt was made to set a limit on the number of people or the number of hours. No restrictions were imposed on the types of weapons that could be brought, such as knives, poles, baseball bats, and aerosol cans. They should at least have banned masks. Nothing. Shocking. The permit was automatically approved on June 13 without a peep out of Charlottesville authorities.

"Here we go, you're not going to believe it," Brian Moran told me as soon as he heard about it. "The alt-right has applied for a permit for a protest in Charlottesville."

"Are you kidding me?" I said to Brian.

I might have added a few choice words in there to show my frustration.

"Sounds like a mess," I said. "What are our options?"

"Tough one," Brian said. "This falls under local jurisdiction, not state, so it's really their call at the local level. I suspect at this point they're more focused on how to balance the demonstrators' First Amendment rights against other concerns. I've got my whole team looking into this. Let's see what they can find."

"This has nothing to do with the Robert E. Lee statue," I said. "Most of these idiots don't even know who the hell Robert E. Lee actually was. They're just using this as a vehicle to come spew their hatred."

As soon as Brian told me, I knew it was going to be bad. He and I talked right away about the need to get our Fusion Center involved. That was our intelligence-gathering agency housed within the Virginia State Police. Fusion Center analysts were experts in gathering information on the alt-right and in developing threat-assessment models. Their work included everything from monitoring social-media sites and chat rooms to sending out undercover agents to provide reliable information on the plans developing for the "Unite the Right" rally.

Ultimately, the key figure for us in our preparations would be Colonel Steve Flaherty, superintendent of the Virginia State Police. At that point he'd already served as superintendent since August 2003, one of the longest tenures in that post in state history, capping a law-enforcement career that began in 1984 when he was hired as a deputy in the Rappahannock County Sheriff's Office. At the time of the September 11, 2001, terrorist attacks, Flaherty was serving as a major in charge of State Police operations and supervised troopers at the Pentagon in the aftermath of the attack. He was superintendent at the time of the horrible 2007 Virginia

Tech massacre, still the deadliest school shooting in history, claiming thirty-two lives. He was in the business of limiting risk and preparing for every possible scenario.

"The Virginia Fusion Center went into hyperdrive mining intelligence, monitoring the groups, monitoring any information we could to determine who might come and what they were planning," Flaherty said later.

The Virginia Department of Emergency Management was led by Jeffrey Stern, a former firefighter, paramedic, and fire battalion chief. Stern had led a team helping New Orleans recover from Hurricane Katrina in 2005, working with teams from other states to reestablish the ravaged city's emergency operations center.

Stern's policy and legislative director was Nicky Zamostny, who had earlier worked for my administration doing policy work and impressed both Brian Moran and me. She'd earned her master's in social work at Virginia Commonwealth University, and had done policy work for us on difficult issues and stood out as a talented, young up-and-comer.

The more we learned about what to expect from the "Unite the Right" rally, the less we liked it. The Fusion Center analysts monitoring online activity found out that these extremist groups were going to be coming from far and wide. Eventually we were told that we'd have alt-right protesters coming to Virginia from all around the country. People were being told to bring weapons. Given Virginia's "open-carry" law, we knew this was going to be an extremely volatile situation.

California-based ProPublica reporter A. C. Thompson was tracking the same alarming trends the Fusion Center was. "When I was reading the white supremacist websites and listening to the podcasts, I could tell they were on board to push this rally in a big way," he later explained. "We've documented a spike in anti-Semitism, a spike in racist graffiti. A real, intense xenophobia. And a connection to Trump. A swastika painted next to a Trump sign. Or somebody saying, 'Trump is going to get rid of you.' . . . There's a feeling that they have the blessing of a sitting president."

We had dozens of people working on preparations for that weekend in August, assessing risk and making plans. We drew up a list of recommendations for Charlottesville to follow to keep people safe that day and also avoid property damage. And then of course I was concerned about how, if things got out of hand, Virginia would be viewed on the world stage. And in a broader sense, what would it mean for America?

As we were preparing for the August "Unite the Right" rally, we got an early taste of what was to come when on July 8 the Ku Klux Klan held a rally in Charlottesville. Fifty North Carolina–based Loyal White Knights of the KKK held a rally in protest of the vote on the Robert E. Lee statue in Charlottesville. Any time you have the KKK marching in broad daylight—some of them in hoods, but most of them not—you have to be concerned. But the reality was, this was—thankfully—a small gathering. As I said at the time, "If you paid no attention to them, nobody would know they're there and they'd probably just stop off at the nearest fast-food joint."

Instead, counterprotesters turned out in huge numbers, easily twenty times the KKK contingent, and so did the Charlottesville Police Department, backed up by the Virginia State Police, Albemarle county police, and University of Virginia police.

"More than a thousand demonstrators flooded this city's downtown Saturday in a display of defiance against a rally by Ku Klux Klan members," *USA Today* reported. "Protesters jeered and booed as around fifty Klan members, some wearing hoods and waving Confederate flags, walked through the streets to gather downtown at Justice Park, escorted by police in riot gear. 'Racists, go home!' they shouted."

You had police actually serving as a buffer between the KKK and the crowd gathered around them, which is what you're supposed to do. The KKK guys were marching out in single file and the counterprotesters were on both sides, telling them to go home. The counterprotesters were furious with the police, yelling at them, "Why are you protecting the KKK?" Then the KKK group had retreated into a parking garage and the counterprotesters wouldn't let them leave. It was at that point it was declared an unlawful assembly and the announcement made for everyone to break it up. Not until State Police threw three canisters of tear gas into that crowd did it disperse enough that the KKK could go home. Police made twenty-two arrests.

"I was pleased with the professionalism and commitment of our law enforcement partners as our safety plan was well executed," Charlottesville Police Chief Al Thomas told reporters. "Officers traveled from near and far to assist the CPD in maintaining law and order during this difficult endeavor."

We learned valuable lessons that day. As Nicky Zamostny noted, "This was when they realized how critical it would be to separate protesters, bus them to the location, and have them enter at different points." But police action that day came with a price. There was a backlash against the arrests and use of tear gas against people standing up to the KKK. The mind-set after that for the Charlottesville City Council was to be wary of any strong law-enforcement presence.

We didn't want a lot of counterprotesters out there, since their presence in large numbers only led to escalation. At the same time, having these racist hatemongers marching in broad daylight was naturally going to stir up some strong reactions in people.

"It's nerve-wracking in a lot of ways," local resident David Straughn told *USA Today*, "but it's something I would regret for the rest of my life if I were not here to face it, to absorb it, to face the trauma that the Klan has caused to people of color, to my own family."

After that small Klan rally in July, the Virginia American Civil Liberties Union (ACLU) sent out letters to four organizations including the Virginia State Police, suggesting that excessive force had been used against those protesting the KKK, calling it an overly militaristic approach. This was a clear warning: Don't do this again. At the state level, we saw that for what it was, just the ACLU being the ACLU, but in Charlottesville it really had city officials nervous.

That was when it started to become clear that we might have an issue with local authorities in Charlottesville being responsive to state officials leading up to the "Unite the Right" rally scheduled for the following month. This was going to be much bigger than anything they'd seen before, with as many as one thousand alt-right protesters. The Charlottesville Police Department had only about one hundred officers at the time and clearly needed backup from State Police, but the rules were clear on who had authority to handle an event like this: the locals. County and state officials were in a support role, and everyone understood that basic dynamic didn't leave much room for telling the locals what to do.

"I just don't get a sense that CPD is preparing adequately," the head of the State Police, Colonel Flaherty, told Brian Moran in mid-July.

Later that month, on July 27, Virginia State Police hosted a briefing at the Fusion Center both to break down what happened in Charlottesville on July 8 and to go over the intelligence we were receiving on how the big "Unite the Right" rally was shaping up. State Police had undercover agents providing us with invaluable data. My communications director, Brian Coy, was part of our team there that day.

"They knew exactly who was coming," Coy remembers. "They

had a good understanding of the tactics we could expect. They were hearing things like that people were hiding bricks around the area they could throw."

My team just wasn't seeing the sense of urgency they wanted to see from local officials, not even when we reached the start of August and the rally was less than two weeks away. They reached the breaking point and decided to call me on vacation to sound the alarm bell.

For years now we've had a McAuliffe family tradition of taking a vacation the first week of August at Smith Mountain Lake, three hours east of Richmond, our five children along with the O'Sheas (five children), the McNerney family (also five), and the Kuhns (two).

On August 2, on the drive back after we played a round at Ballyhack Golf Club, I was riding with Marty McNerney and his son, Conor, when I got an urgent call from Paul Reagan.

"Governor, the city of Charlottesville is just not listening," Paul told me. "This thing is really serious. They're not taking the necessary precautions."

Now I was really alarmed.

"All right, enough of being diplomatic with them," I told Paul. "What do we need to do?"

Colonel Flaherty, Brian, and Paul had worked up a memo for me, breaking down our recommendations. Paul and I decided I'd call Mike Signer, the mayor of Charlottesville, right then to go over the contents of the memo. Marty's and Conor's ears were burning. That was a frank discussion.

Our recommendations were straightforward enough. We urged weapons to be prohibited within ten blocks of the demonstration and suggested other steps like establishing mandatory parking areas and busing in the demonstrators, reducing the time allowance for the protest, and requiring the organizers of the rally to attend a series of mandatory meetings with law enforcement. We also pushed for much better messaging in advance of the demonstration, including a reminder that violence will not be tolerated and that any failure to follow laws would result in immediate arrest.

Date: August 1, 2017
To: Governor McAuliffe
Through: Paul Reagan, Chief of Staff
From: Brian Moran, Secretary of Public Safety and Homeland Security
Re: Conversation with Mayor Michael Signer regarding protests on August 12

Background:
The recommended call is to request that Mayor Signer take aggressive action to fully leverage the City of Charlottesville's permitting authority to ensure the safety and security of protestors and law enforcement. Additionally, the request includes a request for specific messaging from the City of Charlottesville to the groups protesting and general public to outline expectations for civil behavior prior to the event.

The "Unite the Right" rally is scheduled to take place August 12, 2017 from 12PM to 5PM at Lee Park in Charlottesville, Virginia. The rally comes after a particularly divisive spring and summer in Charlottesville, following the city council's vote to remove the Robert E. Lee statue from the downtown park. The event plans to feature multiple "alt-right" and right wing speakers, including Richard SPENCER, Jason KESSLER, Matthew HEIMBACH, Michael HILL, and many others. These groups have espoused beliefs that promote violence.

Per social media and other open source information, over 1,000 (some potentially armed) individuals representing the "alt-right" movement may attend the rally. Conversely, groups opposing the "alt-right" groups (i.e., Black Lives Matter Charlottesville, BlackLivesMatter757, Antifa Seven Hills (ASH), Lynchburg Virginia Antifa, Southern Virginia Antifa, and Showing Up for Racial Justice—Charlottesville) are organizing counter-protests. There have been civil disturbances and acts of violence across the nation at similar events, including in Virginia (July 7).

Talking Points:

I) **Request the City of Charlottesville enhance the requirements/conditions of the permit already provided to the protesting groups, to include:**

- Permit should **not** allow firearms/weapons of any sort within 10 block vehicular restriction area. **Please note:** This requirement could draw attention from pro-Second Amendment groups, so discussion is needed;
- Designated parking areas;
- Bussing protestors to and from protest area. **Please note:** This could set precedent for any future protests;
- Consider reducing time allowance from 5 hours to 3 hours for safety reasons;
- Prohibit signs, poles, items that could be used as weapons;
- Mandatory meetings prior to protest between Law Enforcement and organizers.

2) **Coordinated messaging prior to the event, to include:**

- Consistent message from Charlottesville Government leadership:
- In support of Law Enforcement.
- Violence will not be tolerated/No criminal activity.
- Failure to follow laws will result in immediate arrest.
- Elected Leadership and Law Enforcement supports First Amendment Rights for everyone, which means protesting within bounds of the permit.
- Charlottesville citizens and visitors will be in vicinity enjoying Charlottesville attractions, unruly protests will affect them and could lead to negative experiences, injuries, business disruption.
- Denial of permits for any additional demonstrations on August 12.
- Stress to Mayor, City Manager, Council Members the necessity of meeting with Law Enforcement leadership for situational briefing to understand the potential dynamics of multiple protests in one area.

I went over each of the talking points on the phone with the mayor.

"My State Police are coming to brief you," I said. "It's very important that you listen to them. Colonel Flaherty is very concerned."

As soon as I hung up, I called Paul back and told him I'd gone over the memo with the mayor. I told Paul I thought the call went well, and to get Flaherty and his team over there ASAP. I also mentioned that I was a little concerned that the mayor had asked me if I could bring in some national political figures to hold a counter peace and reconciliation rally. I told him I knew he had good intentions, but I didn't think that was a good idea, since our goal was to limit the number of demonstrators. We didn't want to turn this into a circus.

Three hours later, the Virginia State Police Fusion Center briefed the Charlottesville leadership, covering much of the same material Mike and I had discussed.

"We sent the Fusion Team to Charlottesville to brief the city council," Brian Moran remembers. "That was unprecedented. There's even a picture of the Fusion Center with the mayor and city council to brief them on the seriousness of the threat for violence we faced with this gathering."

City council member Wes Bellamy remembers that meeting well.

"Colonel Flaherty came and I remember him telling us, 'This is what we expect,'" Bellamy told me. "It was serious, like, 'This is what we are dealing with.' A guy said he was bringing the largest white supremacist rally ever seen, coming to my city, and they were targeting me, so you can be sure I was concerned. These people would be bringing weapons. It was just a combustible situation, a kind of perfect storm."

Soon after I'd spoken to the mayor, the State Police came up with another recommendation, which was to move the rally from the very small park where the Robert E. Lee statue stood to right in the middle of downtown. Keeping it there was asking for trouble, since everyone would be crammed in there and law enforcement could not keep the groups separated. Charlottesville authorities had been reluctant to take that step.

We also urged Charlottesville police to use hard barriers to block off traffic flow near the site of the demonstration, which we assumed was a given. Stern's team briefed Charlottesville police on the possibility of a vehicular attack, among other scenarios. Stern had personally seen the aftermath of a vehicular terror attack, a tactic that would later be used elsewhere around the world from Nice to New York.

"Our Incident Management Team briefed at least two dozen of the Charlottesville Police Department that were involved in the leadership about a vehicle attack as a possibility, and the suggestion of the use of hard barriers like dump trucks or buses to prevent vehicles from entering the perimeter," Stern recalls.

There was a lot of discussion of outfitting all police in riot gear, what's known in the trade as a hard look, rather than a soft look, but Charlottesville balked at that. "The city specifically said they did not want a hard look, they wanted a soft look," Nicky Zamostny remembers. "Right or wrong, the philosophy was that if you show up with a militarized look, then these guys say, 'OK, I guess that's what we're doing now.' The hope was that they could keep things at a lower burn by not looking military, more looking civil."

We made our recommendations, knowing we'd get pushback on some but hoping most would be approved. By early the following week, Charlottesville announced they planned to move the demonstration from Emancipation Park to the much larger McIntire Park, which would allow us to have much greater crowd control.

"The size and nature of the demonstration have evolved considerably since the time of Mr. Kessler's application," City Manager Maurice Jones said at a press conference that Monday. "Based on information provided to me by law enforcement officials, the City has decided to approve Mr. Kessler's application for a permit to hold a demonstration on the day and at the times requested, provided that he use McIntire Park, rather than Emancipation Park, for the demonstration. There is no doubt that Mr. Kessler has a First Amendment right to hold a demonstration and to express his views. Nor is there any doubt that we, as a City, have an obligation to protect those rights, the people who seek to exercise them, and the broader community in which they do. We have determined that we cannot do all of these things effectively if the demonstration is held in Emancipation Park."

At the end of his statement, he added—just as we'd been urging—"Finally, I would remind everyone who plans to participate in these demonstrations or counter-demonstrations that you have a right to do so peacefully. You have no right to incite violence or to compromise public safety. I urge everyone to be safe and respectful. We are proud of this community, and we will protect it."

Jason Kessler was not going to make it easy. The "Unite the Right" rally was "absolutely not changing venues," he said. "The genesis of the entire event is this Robert E. Lee statue that the city is trying to move, which is symbolic of a lot of issues that deal with the tearing down of white people's history."

Amazingly enough, both the Virginia ACLU and the Rutherford Institute, a civil liberties organization based in Charlottesville, sent letters to Charlottesville authorities that week in opposition to moving the protest. To me that made no sense. I respect the ACLU and all of the civil-rights advocacy they've done for this country. I'm all for protecting the First Amendment right to freedom of expression, and the ACLU has done great work over the years since it was founded in 1920 by a group including Helen Keller, Jane Addams, and Felix Frankfurter. But on this issue the ACLU should have known better. The First Amendment is not there to protect incitement to violence. My thinking was: If the law enforcement personnel are saying it's no longer a safe situation, then civil libertarians should have stood down. They didn't see it that way.

"While the message of the 'Unite the Right' rally may raise strong feelings of opposition among area residents and political leaders, that opposition can be no basis for government action that would suppress the First Amendment rights of demonstrators who have acted according to the law," the two groups wrote.

Kessler, backed up by those two groups, filed for a preliminary injunction against Charlottesville's decision to move the protest. Representing Kessler in court? None other than the American Civil Liberties Union.

I'd been going on TV and radio late that week imploring the people of Charlottesville, "Please don't go out and counterprotest. Let the police do what they've got to do, but let's not create a bigger problem."

Teresa Sullivan, the president of the University of Virginia, issued a statement advising all students, faculty, and university staff to avoid the rally. "There is a credible risk of violence at this event, and your safety is my foremost concern," she wrote.

I didn't know it then, none of us did, but Sullivan had been hearing rumblings of trouble that went beyond what our State Police intelligence was picking up. Larry Sabato happened to be having dinner that Wednesday night with her. He lived in one of the faculty pavilions right on the Lawn with a view of the Rotunda.

"We were talking about a wide variety of things when the upcoming 'Unite the Right' rally came up," Sabato remembers, and he commented on how a month earlier "a handful of scraggly caricatures showed up with their stars and bars" to march near the Robert E. Lee statue. That wasn't the only concern, Larry found out.

"As we discussed the matter, she raised a concern of which I was unaware—that these far-right characters would somehow end up on the Grounds of the university, maybe on Friday evening,

August 11," Larry recalls. "She may already have had intelligence that this was in the pre-planning stages."

Sabato told her he doubted that would happen.

"They won't want to risk their big Saturday demonstration," he told the university president. "If they take to the campus the night before, they might be arrested and many would be in the pokey on Saturday instead of downtown. They'd miss everything."

Sullivan said she didn't know, but ended the discussion on an ominous note.

"Can you stay at home Friday night?" she asked him. "None of the other Pavilion residents will be around, since the semester hasn't started, and I want a faculty member on hand, just in case."

"Of course," Larry told her, but he couldn't stop thinking about those words, "just in case."

CHAPTER 6

Friday, August 11

. . .

A t 10 a.m. on the Friday morning before the rally we had one last planning meeting in my office at the Patrick Henry Building to review preparations, led by Colonel Flaherty; General Tim Williams, adjutant general of the Virginia National Guard; Brian Moran; and Paul Reagan. No one was more on top of preparations in Charlottesville than Colonel Flaherty. "He'd spent an extraordinary amount of effort as coach and mentor to the police chief in Charlottesville, really going the extra mile to say, 'We need to be thinking about this,' and 'We need to be thinking about that,'" General Williams remembers. "I'm sure there might have come a point in time where he was becoming a lot more blunt, as the event moved closer and closer, but I think it's important that he really went that extra mile."

Jeff Stern briefed us on the outreach his department had done to ensure that emergency teams were in place to include fire personnel and local emergency managers. The University of Virginia medical center was also on alert.

"It was all hands on deck," as Brian Moran put it.

Stern went through a list of his concerns, in order: bombs, like the Boston Marathon bombing; guns; vehicles, like the 2016 Nice attack that killed eighty-seven people, or a vehicle-borne improvised explosive device; fire or Molotov cocktails; chemicals; or finally, cyberattacks. Stern's Incident Management Team had built contingency checklists for each threat. Hazmat teams and fire personnel were on standby in case someone launched chemicals into the crowd. Stern's people would review those preparations with Charlottesville law enforcement later that day.

During that meeting, I ordered General Williams to activate the Virginia National Guard to relocate from Manassas to Charlottesville, but we were going to try to do that without attracting a lot of attention.

"No one is to talk about this," I told everyone at that meeting. "I want this to be kept quiet. If word gets out that the governor has called out the National Guard, every hatemongering lunatic in America will want to be there."

Technically, I ordered the Guard "on standby," as media outlets reported, which was true in a sense, but the Guard wasn't doing much standing that day, they were on the move—and in big numbers.

At the end of that 10 a.m. meeting I turned to Colonel Flaherty and General Williams.

"Do you have everything you need?" I asked Colonel Flaherty.

"Yes, sir, Governor," he said.

"Do you have everything you need?" I asked General Williams.

"Yes, sir, Governor," he said.

"Go do your job."

Our work coordinating with the local police had not gone unnoticed. "As it did with the Klan rally, the Charlottesville police department is coordinating with the Virginia State Police and Albemarle County law enforcement to respond to Saturday's event," that morning's *Washington Post* reported. "The Virginia National Guard issued a statement saying it is monitoring the situation and will 'rapidly respond and provide assistance to local law enforcement if needed to keep citizens safe.'"

No Virginia governor had called out the National Guard for a domestic situation in eighty-five years, not since the Bonus Army crisis of 1932, during the Great Depression, when a large group of World War I veterans marched across the country, starting in Portland, Oregon, demanding deferred pay they'd been promised for their service. Thousands of Bonus Marchers were moving through Virginia on their way to Washington, eventually prompting Governor John Pollard to mobilize the Guard.

In addition to the National Guard, I'd ordered a large contingent of State Police to Charlottesville, but not many people knew. If word had gotten out, that would have been like putting gas on the fire. It would have ignited an already charged atmosphere, and these white supremacists would have been even more fired up to get out there and join in the action.

Our plan almost got blown up. That was a tense afternoon and at one point Brian Coy got a call from Laura Vozzella of *The Washington Post*. She'd been tipped off that someone had seen a lot of National Guard trucks on the road, and she wanted to know if the governor had mobilized the National Guard to Charlottesville. If we confirmed her reporting, it would have been all over the news in no time, escalating the situation. General Williams pointed out we could tell her we had a training exercise ongoing—which in fact was the truth.

"It worked out," remembers General Williams. "Units that had been at Fort Pickett and Fort A.P. Hill were moving, so trucks were up and down the roads, and we were able to deflect that. Because of that, we were able to get the military police company, about 120 people there, staged and set, and then very quietly we were able to get another four hundred and fifty infantry soldiers moved in, which is not easy to do. That's a big footprint. The fact that we didn't turn heads is pretty remarkable."

A. C. Thompson, who would go on to make a *Frontline* documentary, "Documenting Hate: Charlottesville," happened to be on the road toward Charlottesville at the same time as the Guardsmen. "I was driving through the lush Virginia countryside along Route 29 . . . when I saw it: a long convoy of military vehicles, most of them troop carriers," he later wrote. "After a few moments, I realized what was going on. The soldiers were headed south to Charlottesville, where, in a few hours, hundreds of white supremacists were expected to convene for the largest public gathering of racial extremists in decades. I was going there, too, on assignment to cover the rally. Given what had happened in the previous months—three people stabbed at a Klan rally in Anaheim, seven people stabbed at a neo-Nazi event in Sacramento, street fighting that stretched on for hours in Berkeley—I feared it might be a bloody scene in Charlottesville. As the convoy trundled along in the slow lane, I shivered a little despite the heat. The authorities, I thought, must be expecting a storm of violence if they were mobilizing National Guard."

We had everything in place and just hoped there wouldn't be too many issues with coordination and communication. That was always a challenge in situations where you had multiple law enforcement, fire, emergency management, and other entities working together. The state-of-the-art organizational response is a National

Incident Management System, a framework that brings all the parties together under a unified command charged with collectively making operations decisions during an event. In this case the unified command was made up of the Charlottesville City Manager, Charlottesville Police Department, the Charlottesville Fire Department, the University of Virginia Police Department, the Albemarle County Police Department, the National Guard, the State Police, the Virginia Department of Emergency Management, and one FBI agent.

To make it work, you needed buy-in. Everyone has to be all the way on board, not just paying lip service to the idea. In the weeks leading up to Charlottesville, we'd been pushing to have one of our Incident Management Teams provide the planning and logistical support to handle this complex operation, under the direction of an incident commander calling the shots in an emergency situation, though otherwise decisions are made collectively. Finally everyone agreed—but not really.

"When I got down there a day or two ahead of time to check on things," Jeff Stern says, "the city police had put us in a fire station two miles away. It was like, 'Just sit over here, do your plans, great, great.' So it was not truly operating as a system."

We'd passed on intelligence we received about alt-right protesters planting potential weapons in the area around where they expected the rally to be held. That Friday afternoon at 12:32 p.m., NBC 29 reported live on the air that Charlottesville Parks and Recreation had found a long knife hidden in the bushes at Emancipation Park.

Charlottesville Police Chief Al Thomas spoke at a press conference later that afternoon to discuss preparations, explaining that "well over a hundred" Charlottesville police officers and "several hundred officers" from the Virginia State Police would be on hand that weekend.

The press conference took a startling turn at the end. A. C. Thompson asked a question.

"Chief, we're hearing rumors of there being another torchlight march tonight, an unpermitted march, do you have any information about that?" he asked.

"I've heard the same rumors, but I don't have a lot of details," Chief Thomas said. "What have you heard, where is that going to be taking place, the city or the county?"

"Around five or six o'clock," Thompson said.

"Where at?" the Chief asked him.

"Not far from here is what we're hearing," the reporter answered.

Apparently, the Charlottesville Police Department knew at that point that there was going to be a torchlight rally that night, possibly near the UVA Rotunda, and neglected to share that information. We were flying blind on this.

At 5:30 that afternoon, Brian Moran notified me about a reported confrontation in the parking lot of a Walmart in Albemarle County near Charlottesville. Concerned customers had called police to say people were pointing guns in the parking lot. It turned out to be a group of white supremacists including Christopher Cantwell, scheduled to speak at the rally the next day. Cantwell was a blogger and internet radio host who actually convinced people to pay for his content, calling it "common sense extremism." Police came out and checked his open-carry permit, and those of the others, and they were all in order, so no one was arrested.

My schedule called for me to be in Northern Virginia the next morning. They didn't need or want me that Saturday in the Command Center in Charlottesville, where Brian Moran and the whole team would be monitoring events. The last thing you want in a crisis is to have the governor breathing down your neck, telling you what to do. I was relying on my experts. So after careful deliberation, we decided I should carry on and stick to my schedule, drive back to our family home in McLean for the night, and keep in close contact.

Brian Moran had left his office in Richmond that afternoon to get to Charlottesville as soon as he could. He picked up some clothes at home, then drove straight to Emancipation Park in Charlottesville, where he found Colonel Flaherty doing a walk-around. The situation at the park was quiet at that time, and barricades were in place, but Brian was uneasy.

"My first impression was: 'Wow, this park is tiny!'" he remembers.

Colonel Flaherty told Brian he'd heard there might be some kind of alt-right march at UVA. That was the first we were hearing about this. Apparently, people at the university had been in touch with Kessler about some kind of demonstration. We'd reached out to UVA officials often, so it was very disturbing that Flaherty and the rest of our team were only hearing about this then. Brian decided he'd better head over to UVA to see for himself.

"University Police reached out to the alt-right organization," Sullivan later explained in a letter, "and learned early [that] evening that members would be gathering at Nameless Field to march along University Avenue toward the north side plaza of the Rotunda for a short assembly and then disband and depart."

The neo-Nazis said: You can count on us! We're going to behave and not make a spectacle of ourselves. Trust us!

A multi-faith service in opposition to the "Unite the Right" rally was organized for 8 p.m. that night at St. Paul's Memorial Church in Charlottesville, on University Avenue across the street from the UVA Grounds. Dozens of clergy attended the service. Charlottesville's representative in the Virginia House of Delegates, David

Toscano, a former Charlottesville mayor, was there that night. So was Charlottesville City Council member Wes Bellamy.

"The energy in the church was really electric, kind of like before a football game," Bellamy said. "It was like, 'We're not going to let hate win.'"

Here's how Toscano described how events developed: "In a classic case of internet and text-message organizing, 'Unite the Right' participants had gathered in large numbers on short notice at Lambeth Field near the university, and had assembled hundreds of tiki torches, which they ignited, and then proceeded to march about a quarter mile to the Rotunda, passing within five hundred yards of the church. The spectacle of this winding snake of brightly lit tiki torches illuminating the night sky was surreal, taking on the look of a Hitler youth march in the 1930s. The chants were ominous and loud—'Jews will not replace us,' and 'blood and soil.' The word passed quickly that the Nazis and white supremacists were on the march. Fear gripped the church."

Larry Sabato was at home that Friday afternoon, as requested by the UVA president, keeping an eye out on the Rotunda. "By Friday afternoon rumors were flying that there would indeed be some kind of demonstration at the Rotunda come evening," he says. "No one knew the timing, or much of anything else. I received a call around 8 p.m. to be prepared for something in the next hour."

Just after 8 p.m., Richard Spencer texted a *Washington Post* reporter: "I'd be near campus tonight, if I were you. After 9 p.m. Nameless Field."

Larry Sabato was on the Lawn, where there was a lot of activity that afternoon with students moving in for the semester. It's a unique thing about UVA. Fifty-four single rooms are available for a select few students right there on the Lawn, part of Thomas Jefferson's original buildings as part of his vision of an "academical village." The fourth-year honors students who landed those choice rooms were moving in that day, and Larry went out on the Lawn to urge any tourists he found to please leave. Trouble was on the way. Many did leave. The student resident assistant encouraged the new Lawn residents to please find a safer spot. Few did. They wanted to see what was going to happen.

"It had just gotten dark when in the distance, looking west to the mountains, glimmers of lights appeared," Larry told me later. "A well-organized group of neo-Nazis carrying tiki torches was marching and approaching us. It was already clear there were several hundred of them."

Larry was at first astonished, then disgusted and infuriated.

"They were shouting slogans from the Third Reich, like 'Blood and soil,' as well as more contemporary anti-Semitic epithets, like 'Jews will not replace us!' and—horribly—'Into the ovens.'"

Right there on the hallowed Grounds of the University of Virginia, these young fools were calling for Jews to be exterminated. They loved the shock value, these two-bit Hitler admirers, and it was sickening for people to see how brazen they could be with their "Heil Trump!" salutes and Nazi chants. Many, like Charlottesville resident Courtney Commander, used their phones to send out video via social media.

"This looks like the sixties—I wasn't even alive then," Commander said aloud on the video, sent out via Facebook to friends of hers like Heather Heyer, a thirty-two-year-old Charlottesville paralegal.

"You will not replace us!" the goons chanted.

Commander, still shooting video, moved toward them.

"We *will* replace you!" she yelled at them.

There is a firm prohibition against any open flames on the Grounds of the University of Virginia, and normally even one individual carrying a torch could expect campus police to intervene.

Here were hundreds and campus police for some reason took no action. Commander, in her video, raised this point and tried talking to the police.

"Are you guys going to wind up doing something about this?" she asked them. "I'm really not trying to criticize you, but are we allowed to have torches out here?"

Commander had also shot video at the July 8 Ku Klux Klan march in Charlottesville, which had helped her recruit her friends, like Heyer, Marissa Blair, and Marcus Martin, to commit to coming to the August 12 counterprotest. The week before the "Unite the Right" rally, Heyer had told friends she was not going to join the counterprotest because it would be too dangerous, but after watching Commander's video that Friday night, August 11, she was determined to go. "We have to show up in large numbers to show solidarity against the Nazis," she said.

Larry Sabato knew he was living history in a way, as a political scientist, he never imagined he would. Mostly, he said, he was outraged that these idiots who inherited a country built by World War II vets like his father had the nerve to chant such filth as they passed rooms on the UVA Lawn that had been occupied by many who had served.

"I took out my iPhone to take some pictures and record what I was seeing," he says now. "Stupidly, I positioned myself within a yard of them. I was lucky I wasn't hurt."

The student RA had acted quickly, gathering the Lawn residents—starting with Jewish and African American students—to where Larry lived.

"I ordered them down to the basement where they would be safe, with a hidden exit door that could take them away in darkness, if it came to that," he remembers.

Reporter A. C. Thompson was in the middle of the alt-right march.

"'We're gonna put you in camp!' boomed the white supremacist, torch in hand, as he strode past me and my colleague Karim Hajj, a producer and videographer for *Frontline*," he later wrote. "'We're gonna put you in camp!' he shouted again. I didn't know if the words were meant for me, Karim, or just something the guy enjoyed yelling as he marched, a sort of generic all-purpose threat. Other marchers shouted about giving their enemies 'helicopter rides,' an expression meant to evoke the atrocities of Augusto Pinochet, the Chilean fascist ruler whose government thugs had made a habit of hurling the regime's political opponents out of helicopters. The mood of the marchers wasn't merely angry, it felt homicidal."

Brian Moran was at UVA by then. Just after 10 p.m. he texted me a picture of these marchers with their torches and I couldn't believe my eyes. I couldn't believe UVA police didn't immediately arrest and haul off these thugs.

"The neo-Nazis were youngish—teens to thirties— overwhelmingly male, with trained marshals who kept the march- ers in line and chanting in unison," Larry Sabato recalls. "There was a traffic jam as they tried to get from the Lawn to the front of the Rotunda, using the upper plaza."

A group of students and activists gathered at the Jefferson mon- ument in front of the Rotunda to challenge the fanatics and it was clear this was going to get ugly.

"At this point, the fighting broke out, with the Nazis punch- ing and using their torches to stab at a relative handful of students and others who had decided to make a stand, although an unor- ganized one," Larry Sabato says now. "The Nazis got completely out of control—yet the police gathered on the other Rotunda steps in a line of about ten and did nothing."

Activist Emily Gorcenski was in the middle of the fray.

"The Nazis surrounded us very quickly," she said later. "I stood face to face with a man wearing a swastika pin shouting in my face.

1.6.18: Governor Terry McAuliffe with Colonel Steven Flaherty at a memorial fundraiser for the families of Berke Bates and Jay Cullen, Rosie Connolly's Pub, Richmond, VA. *(Courtesy of Jake Rubenstein)*

4.22.16: Governor Terry McAuliffe holding up the signed Executive Order for Restoration of Rights, on the steps of the Virginia Capitol, Richmond, VA. *(Courtesy of Michaele White)*

4.22.16: Governor Terry McAuliffe with one of the people whose rights were restored, on the steps of the Virginia Capitol, Richmond, VA. *(Courtesy of Michaele White)*

4.22.16: Governor Terry McAuliffe signing the Executive Order for Restoration of Rights, on the steps of the Virginia Capitol, Richmond, VA. *(Courtesy of Michaele White)*

7.22.17: Governor Terry McAuliffe and President Donald Trump at the commissioning of the USS *Gerald R. Ford*, Norfolk Naval Station, VA. *(Official Photo)*

5.22.15: Virginia State Police Trooper Berke Bates (far right) with Governor McAuliffe and First Lady Dorothy McAuliffe at Jack McAuliffe's graduation from the Naval Academy in Annapolis, MD. Also in the photo (from left to right) are Virginia State Troopers John Lee Lewis, Patrick Gallagher, and Patrick Green. *(McAuliffe Family Photo)*

Heather Heyer with her mother, Susan Bro, and her stepfather, Kim Bro. Susan says, "We almost never took pictures together because we took for granted that we could do that any time. Here is the last one we took. It was 2016 at my aunt's wedding." *(Courtesy of Susan Bro)*

7.24.17: Governor Terry McAuliffe and Virginia State Trooper Berke Bates at a farewell party at the Executive Mansion, Richmond, VA. Also pictured are Jake Rubenstein, Carrie Caumont, Sally McAuliffe holding Marcello Tiano, and Guinness. *(Courtesy of Michaele White)*

7.22.17: Governor Terry McAuliffe and President Donald Trump during the National Anthem at the commissioning of the USS *Gerald R. Ford*, Norfolk Naval Station, VA. *(Official Photo)*

8.12.17: Governor Terry McAuliffe at the Old Town Alexandria Farmers Market. *(Courtesy of Jake Rubenstein)*

8.13.17: Governor Terry McAuliffe greeting parishioners at a church service in Charlottesville. *(Courtesy of Jake Rubenstein)*

8.13.17: Governor Terry McAuliffe giving remarks at a church service in Charlottesville. *(Courtesy of Jake Rubenstein)*

8.13.17: Governor Terry McAuliffe embracing a parishioner at a church service in Charlottesville. *(Courtesy of Jake Rubenstein)*

8.13.17: Governor Terry McAuliffe at the University of Virginia Trauma Command Center, Charlottesville. *(Courtesy of Jake Rubenstein)*

8.13.17: Governor Terry McAuliffe greeting Lt. Col. Lenmuel S. Terry before addressing the Charlottesville Virginia State Police. *(Courtesy of Jake Rubenstein)*

8.13.17: Governor Terry McAuliffe addressing the Virginia State Police in Charlottesville. *(Courtesy of Jake Rubenstein)*

8.13.17: Governor Terry McAuliffe with officials at the University of Virginia Command Center, Charlottesville. *(Courtesy of Jake Rubenstein)*

8.18.17: Governor Terry McAuliffe with members of the hockey team that Trooper Pilot Berke Bates coached. They are pictured at his funeral at Saint Paul's Baptist Church, Richmond, VA. *(Courtesy of Jake Rubenstein)*

8.18.17: Governor Terry McAuliffe signing Executive Order 67, which stopped the issuance of permits and prohibited demonstrations at the Lee Monument. Photo taken with Counsel Noah Sullivan in the Old Governor's office at the Executive Mansion under the photo of civil rights attorney Oliver Hill. *(Courtesy of Jake Rubenstein)*

8.19.17: Governor Terry McAuliffe consoling Karen Cullen before the funeral for her husband Lieutenant Jay Cullen at the Southside Church of Nazarene, Chesterfield, VA. *(Courtesy of Jake Rubenstein)*

8.24.17: Governor Terry McAuliffe in his office signing Executive Order 68 establishing the Task Force on Public Safety Preparedness and Response to Civil Unrest. Also pictured (clockwise from the Governor): Deputy Secretary for Homeland Security and Public Safety Curtis Brown, Secretary of the Commonwealth Kelly Thomasson, Deputy Secretary of the Commonwealth Traci Deshazor, and Assistant Secretary of Public Safety and Homeland Security Nicky Zamostny. *(Courtesy of Jake Rubenstein)*

8.27.17: Governor Terry McAuliffe and First Lady Dorothy McAuliffe at a reception at the Executive Mansion for Bon Air Juvenile Correctional Center Family Day. Also pictured: Department of Juvenile Justice Director Andy Block (far left) and Secretary of Public Safety and Homeland Security Brian Moran (far right). *(Courtesy of Michaele White)*

12.12.16: Governor Terry McAuliffe and First Lady Dorothy McAuliffe with Berke and Amanda Bates and their children, Kylie and Deacon, at the annual holiday party for members of the Governor's Executive Protection Unit. *(Courtesy of Michaele White)*

12.12.16: Governor Terry McAuliffe and First Lady Dorothy McAuliffe with Jay and Karen Cullen and their children, Ryan and Max, at the annual holiday party for members of the Governor's Executive Protection Unit. *(Courtesy of Michaele White)*

Governor Terry McAuliffe in 2017, the last time he saw Berke Bates. *(Personal photo)*

Governor McAuliffe with Berke Bates, disembarking from Trooper 1, piloted by Jay Cullen. *(Courtesy of Michaele White)*

Terry McAuliffe with President Bill Clinton visiting Nelson Mandela in South Africa. *(Official Photo)*

I was ready to die that night. I figured that was just how it was going to go. Earlier in the day I had written my final messages to the ones I loved in case I didn't make it through the weekend. I don't know who threw the first punch. When it got violent, the circle shifted to one side and we were able to run."

That was about when Sabato ran into Brian Moran, who was on the phone briefing Colonel Flaherty.

"It was wild," Brian says. "They were taking the torches and throwing the torches up in the air. It was unbelievable, watching this. You look around and all you think is, 'What is this, 1938 in Germany? *Kristallnacht*?' It turned out, Larry Sabato was standing right next to me."

They exchanged information and were tempted to take a break.

"Let's go back to my office and have a shot of bourbon," Larry suggested.

It was more gallows humor than a serious offer.

"No bourbon tonight," Brian said. "I better keep my wits about me."

Finally the UVA police moved in. Both Brian and Larry were struck at how organized the neo-Nazis were. They'd clearly been training for this moment—and Kessler's so-called promise not to march meant authorities were caught off guard, though as Brian put it, "Obviously Kessler and the others were lying." As Larry put it, "Since when does anybody trust the word of Nazis?"

"It was exactly like what you'd see in a World War II documentary of Nazi Germany," Brian said later. "I had never seen anything like that. It just shakes you. It was surreal to see. And the youth, how young these people were. I was just bracing for what might unfold the next day."

Larry Sabato waited for the crowd to disperse and left with the dean of students, who had been stabbed with a tiki torch. "Everyone was in a daze and the students around me were badly shaken," he says. "Terry Sullivan asked me to stay on the Lawn day and night for the rest of the weekend, just in case."

Brian called Sullivan that night around 11 P.M.

"I'm really afraid with what's going on this weekend," she told him.

Just after 9 p.m., the news broke that U.S. District Judge Glen Conrad had issued a ruling blocking Charlottesville's petition to move the next day's rally to McIntire Park, meaning it would be back at Emancipation Park as originally planned. I was stunned to hear the decision. That to me was just unconscionable. The judge was explicitly tossing out the notion that the city wanted to make the move for public safety. That's a hell of a gamble to make. What if people end up dying because of your choice? What good is it going to do them then to talk about public safety factors not being relevant?

Worst of all, the judge came right out and said he was blaming City Council members for posts on social media that showed they were against these right-wing extremists. "This conclusion is bolstered by other evidence, including communications on social media indicating that members of City Council oppose Kessler's political viewpoint," Conrad wrote.

Now, wait a minute. How does opposing Kessler's hate-filled extremist viewpoint rule out a need to act on behalf of public safety? These people were coming armed and dangerous. None of this made any sense.

Claire Guthrie Gastañaga, executive director of the ACLU of Virginia, seemed thrilled by the ruling.

"We encourage everyone participating to commit to nonviolence and peaceful protest," she said.

You can be sure that the alt-right types converging on Charlottesville from around the country read those words and laughed until they couldn't laugh anymore. Nonviolence? Peaceful protest? Yeah, right.

She added: "We will be there to observe and document police practices." Nothing about documenting the behavior of thugs gathered to hurt people and spew hate.

(We weren't the only ones scratching our heads over why the ACLU had gone to bat for the white supremacists. Two months later, angry students would show up at a talk on First Amendment issues by Claire Guthrie Gastañaga. The protesters made it very difficult for her to speak, chanting "ACLU, you protect Hitler, too," and "Blood on your hands!" and "ACLU, free speech for who?" Later they posted a statement: "In contrast to the ACLU, we want to reaffirm our position of zero tolerance for white supremacy no matter what form it decides to masquerade in.")

That night set the tone for the weekend. The banner headline in the next morning's Charlottesville *Daily Progress* blared FIRE AND FURY in huge letters and that pretty well summed up the sense of horror and outrage so many of us felt.

My deputy communications director, Heather Fluitt, followed the night's lurid images via social media, like so many others. She was deeply shaken. "That was the first real picture of the kind of people that had come into Virginia, the depth of evil and disconnectedness that these people felt and displayed," she says now. "I don't think any of us were expecting that to take place that night. It was sort of a preview of what was to come the next day. It was very stark to see that, and very shocking. It certainly raised the alarm bells for me and for all of us."

Watching on TV at home in McLean, Dorothy and I couldn't believe this was happening in our home state in the year 2017. So many out-of-state agitators had come in to defile everything we cared about. It was disgusting and infuriating. The torchlight rally at UVA served notice of what we could expect the next day near the Robert E. Lee statue. We felt a growing sense of dread.

"Many of the individuals coming to Charlottesville are doing so in order to express viewpoints many people, including me, find abhorrent," I'd emphasized in a statement released earlier that day. "As long as that expression is peaceful, that is their right. But it is also the right of every American to deny those ideas more attention than they deserve. Men and women from state and local agencies will be in Charlottesville tomorrow to keep the public safe, and their job will be made easier if Virginians, no matter how well-meaning, elect to stay away from the areas where this rally will take place."

CHAPTER 7

Saturday Morning, August 12

. . .

We'd made all the preparations we could at the state level, and had full mobilization of our State Police and National Guard, but I remained apprehensive about what the day would bring. Brian Moran started calling and texting me with updates at 6:30 that morning. He and his deputy, Curtis Brown, attended a 7 a.m. briefing for law enforcement and first responders at the John Paul Jones Arena, where Department of Corrections buses were lined up to take our troopers to downtown Charlottesville.

"I let them know we had the potential for violence, that while precious few of us were from there or ever lived there, that Charlottesville was our city that day," Colonel Flaherty said later.

Brian called the Charlottesville mayor at 7:15 a.m. to check in with him. We wanted to make sure the mayor was well aware that we were mobilized in force and ready to do anything we could in support. Next, Brian and Curtis, along with Colonel Flaherty, drove over to a downtown garage. As they were pulling off the ramp onto the third level, they saw a group of heavily armed men in fatigues exiting their vehicles.

"They ain't ours?" Brian said to Curtis.

They both shook their heads and braced for the rest of the day. Brian was in place at the corner of Emancipation Park at 8:35 a.m. when he watched the first alt-right types arrive and assemble, some in helmets, carrying shields and flagpoles. Jason Kessler's permit called for a rally between noon and 5 p.m., and the marchers were already massing this early in the morning.

Brian stood within a few feet to listen in on their chants and conversation to glean any information he could on how they were organizing. He tried to identify as many different militia insignia as he could. All around him the crowd of young white males grew. Soon they were lining both sides of the street.

Gay Lee Einstein, a pastor at nearby Scottsdale Presbyterian Church who lived in Charlottesville, was part of a gathering of hundreds of clergy heading toward the rally that morning. She told me she'd found a plastic baggie full of rocks and a white piece of paper warning of "Shocking crime facts" and signed by the Ku Klux Klan, closing, "Wake up, white America!" She stayed with the group as long as she could. "I started crying during the thing," she told me.

Eileen, a registered nurse who was volunteering that day to help out as she could, was with the group of clergy near Emancipation Park that morning. "I was in the middle of all of it," she told me later. "We watched the crowd grow. I saw a lot of aggressive sexism toward young women. I saw a lot of woman being called the C-word and being mistreated. One woman was a little on the chubby side and these men were saying things like, 'You're a little fat, but we'd still do you.' I was so perplexed by it all, I went back and studied it. When hate wants to find something to hate, they just kind of change their target."

Around 10 a.m., I was keeping an eye on my phone, ready for the latest from Brian, and he sent me a picture of a heavily armed militia marching into the park in formation, like they owned the place. They were so loaded up, they looked like extras in a *Rambo* movie. It was a very disturbing picture. Brian gave me a full report on these militia men in camouflage gear with large semi-automatic weapons and extra ammo slung over their shoulders.

"Governor, these guys have better weapons than our State Police," Brian told me sarcastically.

"Who the hell are they?" I asked.

"I don't know," he said.

"Well, go find out," I told him.

So Brian walked over and tried to talk to these guys. I could hear most of what was said, since he was holding his phone and still had me on the line. The first militia member he approached was unresponsive, so Brian introduced himself as the secretary of public safety and tried another one. This time, the militia member was more talkative. He explained that his group was there to protect the First Amendment (and, obviously, the Second). It went so well, Brian decided to look for the leader of the group and try to negotiate a truce or at least understand what this militia saw as its role that day. The next member he approached refused to talk to him.

"I can't talk to you, sir," he said. "You have to talk to my CO, sir!"

So that was how it was going to be. For us it was one more element of insanity to have all these guys walking around in camouflage uniforms with revolvers strapped to their sides and huge semi-automatic weapons. It was surreal. We didn't know why they were there—and I'm not sure they did either.

It turned out this was one of many right-wing militia groups that showed up that day, including the Pennsylvania Light Foot Militia, the New York Light Foot Militia, and the Virginia Minutemen Militia. They were well organized, well armed—and intimidating—and said they were against both sides, neo-Nazis and counterprotesters. One of the militia leaders dismissed both sides as "jackasses."

"The show of strength was about 'allegiance . . . to the Constitution,' particularly the First Amendment, said Christian Yingling, leader of the Pennsylvania Light Foot Militia," *The Washington Post* reported. "He said he and his troops 'convoyed in' to Charlottesville early Saturday to defend free speech by maintaining civic order so everyone present could voice an opinion, regardless of their views. . . . 'We put our own beliefs off to the side,' Yingling said. 'Not one of my people said a word. They were given specific orders to remain quiet the entire time we were there. . . . Our mission was to help people exercise their First Amendment rights without being physically assaulted.'"

This was the largest white-nationalist gathering in the United States in decades, and the neo-Nazis and other fanatics were giddy. They were having the time of their lives. "The white nationalists were so young," Pastor Viktória Parvin of St. Mark Lutheran Church in Charlottesville said later. "They were laughing, like they were going to a party."

Naturally, David Duke, the former grand wizard of the Ku Klux Klan, was there. He grinned and beamed to well-wishers. "This represents a turning point for the people of this country," Duke said that morning. "We are determined to take our country back. We are going to fulfill the promises of Donald Trump, and that's what we believed in. That's why we voted for Donald Trump, because he said he's going to take our country back."

The crowd loved it. They were whipped up into a frenzied state. They yelled at an African American woman that they'd put her on the "first f— boat home" and told any white person standing side by side with an African American they were going "straight to hell," finishing with a Nazi salute.

The words these marchers were spewing were unbelievable. Profane, disgusting, infuriating. It's worth remembering that nobody is born with the hatred that these people spewed. Nor were they representative of American values. We're a nation of 328 million people, so let's not lose sight of the fact that these were a thousand people marching, a small, fringe element pulled together from thirty-five different states. They came out of the woodwork. They came out of their cellars. This was going to be a great day for them. This event had been hyped so much, especially after the torchlight march the night before; everyone in the world knew about this rally.

There were so many different groups and uniforms, it was confusing. There were huge Confederate flags and huge red flags carrying the swastika of the Nazis. There were patches with swastikas and Confederate flags. At times, it was hard to tell whether the alt-right marchers were directing their hate more at black people or more at Jews. "As Jews prayed at a local synagogue, Congregation Beth Israel, men dressed in fatigues carrying semi-automatic rifles stood across the street, according to the temple's president," *The Atlantic* reported. "Nazi websites posted a call to burn their building. As a precautionary measure, congregants had removed their Torah scrolls and exited through the back of the building when they were done praying."

Hard to believe this was 2017, not 1937. I was very concerned about the weaponry Brian was observing out there. The marchers were carrying semi-automatic weapons, pistols, long guns, all legal under Virginia's open-carry law. It's scary enough to see one man standing on a street corner with a long gun, but scary as hell when you put hundreds of men with semi-automatic weapons together in a small space. My biggest fear was that if some hot-head started firing shots, all hell would break loose and we'd have dozens of body bags.

I was at home watching on cable television and they started showing a lot of fights. The world was convinced that pandemonium had taken over the streets of Charlottesville. It looked like the entire place was a melee. They kept replaying the same skirmishes over and over, and for a lot of people watching it looked worse than it actually was, but it was clearly a dangerous, volatile situation that could get out of hand in a hurry.

At 10:06 a.m., I called Colonel Flaherty to get his take.

"Governor, there's a lot of action downtown," he said. "I'm very concerned with the way things are going."

After dealing with Colonel Flaherty for three and a half years, I knew what he was trying to tell me—things are about to blow.

I knew it was time to start thinking about declaring a state of emergency and dispersing the gathering, so at 10:21 a.m. I called AG Mark Herring; my counsel, Carlos Hopkins; and Lieutenant Governor Ralph Northam to put them on notice that I was preparing to declare a state of emergency.

As bad as the clips made it look, up until that point what we were seeing on the ground was more or less in line with what we'd expected. When you've got a thousand people gathered, carrying sticks, many of them spoiling for a fight, there are going to be incidents. There is going to be some pushing and shoving. There are going to be some skirmishes and fights. The reality was that this could swing either way.

The key to controlling a protest is always keeping the different groups separated. That would have been a lot easier at McIntire Park, but because of the ACLU and one judge, this roiling mix of thousands of demonstrators and counterprotesters was all packed into a small area in and around Emancipation Park. The Charlottesville police's plan, unfortunately, relied at least in part on the honor system and the hope that the neo-Nazis would do what they'd said they would do. It didn't work out that way. No surprise.

"Charlottesville Police Chief Al S. Thomas Jr. said the rally goers went back on a plan that would have kept them separated from the counterprotesters," *The Washington Post* reported. "Instead of coming in at one entrance, he said, they came in from all sides. Headlong into the counterprotesters. A few minutes before 11 a.m., a swelling group of white nationalists carrying large shields and long wooden clubs approached the park on Market Street. About two dozen counterprotesters formed a line across the street, blocking their path. With a roar, the marchers charged through the line, swinging sticks, punching and spraying chemicals."

Reporter A. C. Thompson was in the middle of the action. "We witnessed one instance where a battalion of white supremacists encountered an older group of counterprotesters," he said later. "They were like give-peace-a-chance, middle-aged and senior-citizens kind of folks. And the white supremacists just absolutely pummeled them."

Eileen the nurse was nearby, treating anyone who came into her tent. At one point a leader of one of the groups was hit by pepper spray and came stumbling into her tent. "He was trying to radio his buddies to tell them what to do," she recalls. "My husband said, 'This is Switzerland, we will treat you, but you have to put that radio down.' He finally did. But he wouldn't stop crying and screaming, 'My eyes, my eyes!'"

Our folks had reviewed a long list of contingency plans and underlined the importance of sealing off the streets around the park. That was basic crowd control, less a question of specific threat assessment, but that Saturday the measures taken were inadequate. A single wooden sawhorse was all that stood in the way of cars driving down Fourth Street, a barrier that a Prius could plow through without much of an issue. At the corner of Market Street and Fourth Street NE, the way was blocked by a single officer stationed there.

It was all sliding toward pandemonium, as Brian Moran watched from the command center on the sixth floor of the Wells Fargo building, giving me constant updates. "That was when the crowd converged into chaos," Brian remembers. "The access to the park was all messed up. In addition to the incredible naïveté that they would even follow such a plan, there were way too many protesters to follow such instructions. The park fencing was just too small to accommodate the crowds of either supremacists or counterprotesters. The design was just flawed. It required the two groups to interact."

The main issue on declaring a state of emergency was one of protocol. As I've outlined, the default is always for local control and local decision-making. So normally, the city would be the one to declare an unlawful assembly, and that was what Colonel Flaherty was expecting. He saw it as the call of the Charlottesville police chief, Al Thomas. Brian Moran was going out of his mind trying to sort it all out.

"I'm in this window on the sixth floor looking down at what was happening below, and the command center was on the other side of the building; they were overlooking the Mall, so they weren't even eyes-on," he says. "So I kept running from this window to the other end of the hall, grabbing Flaherty, and saying, 'What the hell! You've got to make the call that it's time for the governor to declare a state of emergency. This is crazy out there. It's gotten bad.'

But he was waiting on Thomas to give him the signal, because the city wanted to issue their declaration first."

Flaherty was in a tough position, and everyone knew it. Law enforcement always wanted to respect law enforcement, and follow chain of command, but Brian had seen enough.

"Steve, this can't go on any longer," he told Flaherty. "Soon after, my phone rang."

At just after 11:15 a.m. my phone rang.

"Governor, you've got to declare a state of emergency," Brian said. "This is out of control. I'm seeing bottles being thrown. They look like Molotov cocktails. We can't wait for Charlottesville. Screw protocol."

I didn't need to think about it at all—not for half a second. I'd seen enough. It was time for decisive action.

"That's it," I said. "Send 'em in! Send in the State Police. Send in the Guard. Clear the damn park."

The record reflects that at 11:28 a.m., via text message, I confirmed that I had authorized a state of emergency. Immediately after my action, at 11:29, the city declared it an unlawful assembly.

A BearCat armored vehicle was moved into position. The Virginia State Police tactical teams—everyone outfitted in riot gear—got on bullhorns and at 11:32 declared it an unlawful assembly and notified protesters that they were clearing the park. The event was canceled and everyone had eleven minutes to leave.

At 11:43, exactly eleven minutes after the announcement, Virginia State Police tactical teams moved into place and cleared the park. By noon the Virginia National Guard had followed the tactical teams in and secured the park.

The rally ended just before it was officially scheduled to begin at noon. We'd made it through with some minor injuries and no property damage. There had been no looting and no windows smashed. No destruction of property. We were relieved. There was nothing else for me to do at that point. It was over, we all thought and hoped.

CHAPTER 8

Saturday Afternoon, August 12

. . .

My phone rang with a call from the White House.

"Is this Governor McAuliffe?" a woman's voice asked.

"Yes," I said.

"This is Operator One at the White House, the president would like to speak to you."

"Great," I said.

"We'll call back in five minutes with the president," she said.

This was the call I'd been expecting. That's what you do as president, you call the state governor in a time of emergency.

"What is going on?" Trump asked me.

"We've got a real mess on our hands, Mr. President," I said.

As I explained in the opening pages of this book, I gave Trump the details of the situation on the ground and told him that my secretary of public safety and homeland security, Brian Moran, had been on-site giving me regular briefings since 6:30 in the morning. I told him that we had cleared Emancipation Park and felt like we were getting a handle on the situation, but that these neo-Nazis and white supremacists were a horrible group of individuals and we still had a dangerous, volatile situation on our hands. I used the opportunity to speak out against Trump's anti-immigrant rhetoric.

"Mr. President, the way to move forward is to bring people together and stop the hate speech," I said. "This rhetoric coming out of the White House is bad for the country. We've worked hard here for three and a half years, our economy in Virginia is humming, we've got unemployment from 5.4 percent down to 3.8 percent. All this stirring people up on race is wrong and it's going to hurt our economy. We've got to stop this hatred in America."

He said he agreed, but I had the strange feeling he didn't hear half of what I had said. He ignored my urgent words on hatred and race-baiting and focused just on the economy. In fact, he went off on a long tangent about how great the national economy was doing under his leadership and how African American unemployment was at a historic low. I kept quiet and did not point out that he was riding on the momentum that President Obama had built up with a record seventy-five consecutive months of job growth after the devastation of the 2008 Great Recession. As I hung up the phone, I was hoping the president would take my words to heart.

Not much later, Brian Moran called me from Charlottesville.

"Governor, have you got the TV on?" he asked me. "I've got bad news. Some idiot just ran his car into the crowd. A lot of people have been injured."

I was stunned.

"Anybody killed?" I asked.

"We don't know yet. It's bad, Governor. There are a lot of injuries. Some people are in pretty bad shape."

Twenty-year-old James Alex Fields Jr. of Maumee, Ohio, had driven his Dodge Challenger at high speed and rammed into a crowd of people near Emancipation Park, and then thrown it into reverse and sped off. At that point we did not know the details. We did not yet know that thirty-two-year-old Heather Heyer, a peaceful protester, had been murdered by this act of domestic terrorism. We did not know that the number of other people injured when Fields hit the gas in a spirit of hate would ultimately rise to thirty-five. This was a self-professed neo-Nazi who had literally texted his mother a picture of his hero Adolf Hitler the day before with the clear threat: "We're not the one who need to be careful."

The State Police helicopter I normally used was overhead at the time of the attack on a surveillance mission with my pilot, Jay Cullen, and Berke Bates, who'd grown so close to our family as part of our EPU.

"The helicopter was above it, so we had a real-time, live view of it in the command post," Colonel Flaherty said later. "We knew immediately."

It was a horrific scene in the aftermath of Fields's terrorist attack. "I remember the sounds," A. C. Thompson, there on the scene, would remember. "Moaning and screaming. Helicopters whirling overhead. The wailing of ambulance sirens."

Graphic designer Kristin Adolfson, a UVA alum, told *The New Yorker* she was ten feet away when the car came barreling through.

"We were just marching, being peaceful," she said. "It was a very exuberant feeling of solidarity, community, all that. We decided to turn up Fourth Street, to go back to the downtown Mall. . . . I still don't know how a car got down there. Then I heard shouts and this sound of, like, hitting, like, traffic cones. This hollow, horrible sound. Like dominoes. And I saw bodies fly up into the air. People were running away. And then the car backed up. I didn't know what was going on. We were all running away. . . . Someone told me a person was dead. It took a while for the ambulance to get there. People were wailing. Like, really wailing in a way I've never heard. It was horrible. It was horrible. It was horrible.

I was ten feet away, so I didn't really see details of the car. It was just sudden movement through the crowd, sound, bodies in the air. . . . This was a terrorist act. Something that happens in so many places around the world, and it happened here in our little town. It was hard to process that. And the hate—that someone could actively take people's lives, that's what their goal was."

Trooper 1 helped track the neo-Nazi terrorist in his Dodge Challenger, with Jay piloting and Berke surveilling. "The helicopter stayed with the car," Colonel Flaherty said later. "They followed it and then the sheriff's department made the stop. We watched that unfold from the downlink. . . . [Berke] captured an incredible video that shocked us in the command post. He captured that pursuit. That is great evidence."

Heather Heyer had held firm on her choice to attend the counterprotest, despite her concerns about potential violence, and joined her friends Courtney Commander and Marissa Blair, both fellow paralegals, and Marissa's fiancé, Marcus Martin. That afternoon, word was relayed to Heather's mother, Susan Bro, that authorities at a local hospital wanted to speak to Heather's "next of kin." Which authorities? Which hospital? Susan didn't know. She called both hospitals in town, asking about her daughter, and both told her, "We don't have a patient by that name."

"That was very frustrating," Susan told me later. "My son had seen the incident on TV and he called his sister's phone. A stranger picked up and said they found it on the sidewalk. They didn't know who his sister was or where she was."

Susan also called her parents.

"You'd better pray," she told them, "but the fact they're asking for next of kin tells me she's unconscious or worse."

Susan found the right hospital, the same hospital where she'd given birth to Heather thirty-two years earlier. "I look at so much of her life now, it feels like full circle," she says. "Where she died is just a few miles from where she was conceived, a few miles from where she was born, a few miles from where she lived when she was killed; it's all there within a few miles of each other, and yet her death had an impact worldwide."

Some comfort came that day when Susan asked a detective what her daughter had been doing when she was killed.

"She was with a group of peaceful counterprotesters," she was told.

Susan was asked if she wanted to come in to see the body and she said, "Not until my husband gets here." By the time he arrived, Heather's body had already been taken away to the medical examiner's office in Richmond.

Susan thought back to her recent meal with Heather at the Wood Grill Buffet on Branchlands Boulevard. "We spent the whole meal talking about social injustice and racism, just life in general, as mothers and daughters often do," Susan told me. "Every once in a while I would get in a comment. She was just a very animated talker, and talked with her hands a lot. We didn't talk about the rally coming up."

They finished and headed out to the car.

"It was so strange, because when we went outside, I remember we hugged harder than usual and we kissed each other on the cheek," Susan told me. "We were laughing about it, saying, 'It's not like we'll never see each other again, good grief.' And yet, we never did. We never saw each other again. The next time I saw her was when I identified the body the day before the funeral."

I knew, after Heather Heyer's death, that I had to get to Charlottesville in a hurry. Since Trooper 1 was in use, Fairfax 1, a Fairfax county helicopter, was going to fly me down. I was in the kitchen at home watching when Trump gave his press conference from his country club in Bedminster, New Jersey, that afternoon. When he said there was hatred, bigotry, and violence "on many sides," I was outraged—and knew I had to speak up. I immediately had a conference call with my press team.

"I have to hold a press conference," I said. "Somebody has got to address this. Somebody has to speak for the nation."

I called Dorothy at 3:29 p.m. to let her know I was being flown to Charlottesville in a helicopter. That was my last call before I climbed in and we took off at 4:03, landing at 4:45. My phone had died, and I had no way to charge it until I landed, so I was out of communication for about fifty minutes.

"There's your helicopter, there's Trooper 1," the Fairfax county pilot told me as we were about to land in a field outside Charlottesville, pointing to the scanner.

After I landed I hopped into my car and drove in a large motorcade. There was a huge contingent of State Police cars accompanying me, given the events of the day. Local officials in Charlottesville had announced a press conference, and my team told them to hold off until I arrived, so we were in a hurry to get there. As we were driving, we heard "aircraft down" on police radio, and I had a sinking feeling.

I didn't know what to think. There weren't many aircraft in the air at all. Your first thought is you hope no one is hurt, and the worst part is, you hate not knowing. You have to wait for more details. I had enough bad news to occupy my thoughts without wondering about unknowns.

We stopped by the Charlottesville command center and they escorted me up into a conference room to await the press conference. I knew I was going to have to take a strong stance against these neo-Nazis who had invaded our state, and I tried to stay focused on what I would say, but for the thirty minutes I waited, I was so worried that it was our helicopter that went down.

Meanwhile, up in Richmond, my staff had gotten word that a helicopter was down. No one was able to reach me for twenty minutes, since my phone was dead, and they were in a panic. Everyone was asking: "Was that the governor's helicopter that crashed?" I didn't know about any of that until much later.

A few minutes later in the conference room where I was waiting, Marc Wiley, the head of my EPU, came over to give me the news.

"Governor, the aircraft that went down?" he said. "It was ours."

"And Jay and Berke?" I asked him.

"We don't know," he said.

There are moments you never forget and that was one of them. I let out a huge sigh and slumped down and stared at the table. I was frozen for a moment, having a hard time believing it really could be true.

"I saw the look on the governor's face when he got that news," my deputy press secretary, Heather Fluitt, remembers. "He was devastated. I had never seen him so sad. It was very clear his heart was broken by what he had just heard."

My thoughts were racing. I thought of both Jay and Berke, all the times we'd joked around together, all the talks we'd had, all the kindness they'd shown my family. Peter and Sally, I knew, would be crushed. Jay was forty-eight, and Berke forty. They both had beautiful families and were dedicated to their wives and children. It was just so heartbreaking, such a tragedy.

I'm not one who has a lot of trouble focusing, especially not in the middle of an emergency, but I'll tell you the truth. Standing in that room, getting ready to go out and speak to the cameras, a part of me just wanted to stand there and remember my friends Jay and Berke.

I was angry and I was sad, but I knew the whole world was looking at our state, wondering, "Who *are* you?" I needed to tell them who we were. And I needed to call these people out for who they were. They were neo-Nazis and white supremacists and I was going to call them out as neo-Nazis and white supremacists. No one else wanted to do that, but I was only too glad to do it. Trump had spoken and come up small. It fell to me to speak for what people everywhere were feeling about the tragic day in Charlottesville. I knew I was speaking to the nation, and I felt like I was speaking to the world.

We headed to the municipal center for the press conference. I was escorted into the holding room and it looked like everyone in the Charlottesville city government was there, from the mayor to the city manager to the police chief and different City Council members, all of them wanting to come over and talk to me about the day's events.

It was hard. When Marc first told me Trooper 1 was down, I didn't know for sure that Jay and Berke were dead. There didn't seem to be much room for hope, but you always hold on. By the time we were in the holding room, they had recovered the bodies and I got word that we had lost them both. And the worst part was, I couldn't announce their deaths to the public at that point—not until we'd been able to notify the families. So if I was asked about the helicopter crash, I'd have to be as vague as I could.

I had to call Dorothy. The office tried to reach her when they couldn't figure out if I was in the downed aircraft that was reported. Dana Estrada, her EPU detail that day, was in touch with State Police on the ground in Charlottesville.

Dorothy recounted that horrible moment.

"Dana and I knew a helo was down—we knew it wasn't the one Terry was in, but we knew it was Trooper 1," she remembers. "Two trooper pilots were down, but we didn't know which pilots. We were both in shock."

Minutes later I got Dorothy on the phone. It was hard to say the words.

"There was a helicopter crash and Jay and Berke were killed," I told her.

I called just as she and Dana had heard the news from State Police, and she was having trouble speaking through the tears.

She said she would call our older children to give them the news—Dori in New York, Jack in Iraq, and Mary in Tel Aviv. Dorothy was going home to get Peter and our new puppy, and head to Richmond right away. We needed to be together as a family.

"I know, I know," I said. "When I get back to Richmond, I'm going to see Amanda and Karen, but first I will stop by the mansion so I can be the one to tell Sally."

Seconds after I hung up with Dorothy, I was out there speaking to the cameras. I stepped up to the podium and spoke from the heart with no notes. I delivered the following remarks:

In addition to many individuals who have been hurt, let me start off first by thanking all of our law enforcement officials. This could have been a much worse day today. I want to thank our local law enforcement individuals. I want to thank the first responders. I want to thank all the State Police, the National Guard, and everybody else who was involved in today's activities. We planned for a long time for today's incidents.

I also want to give a special thank you to the clergy who were here today who helped us on the streets. I also want to thank those courageous UVA college students yesterday who last evening surrounded the statue of Thomas Jefferson to protect that statue.

And I have a message to all the white supremacists and the Nazis who came in to Charlottesville today. Our message is plain and simple. Go home. You are not wanted in this great commonwealth. Shame on you.

You pretend that you're patriots, but you are anything but a patriot. You want to talk about patriots? Talk about Thomas Jefferson and George Washington, who brought our country together.

You think about the patriots today, the young men and women who are wearing the cloth of our country. Somewhere around the globe they are putting their life in danger. They're patriots. You are not.

You came here today to hurt people and you did hurt people. But my message is clear. We are stronger than you. You have made our commonwealth stronger. You will not succeed. There is no place for you here, there is no place for you in America.

We work here today to bring people together, to unify folks. I'll remind you all that we are a nation of immigrants. Unless you're Native American, the first ships that came to Jamestown, Virginia, in 1607, and since that time, many people have come to our great country to unite us.

Our diversity, that mosaic tile of immigrants, is what makes us so special, and we will not let anybody come here and destroy it. So please go home and never come back. Take your hatred and take your bigotry. There is no place.

And if I could give you a piece of advice, use your time and energy to help people. Come with me to a homeless shelter. Come with me to help a veteran find a job or a place to live. That's what we need help on, to bring people together.

I spoke to the president this afternoon, and we had a conversation and I told the president that there has got to be a movement in this country to bring people together.

The hatred and rhetoric that has gone on and has intensified over the last couple months is dividing this great nation.

We need to work together. I told the president that twice, be willing to work with you if we can work together to bring people together, but stop the hate speech. Stop the rhetoric in this country. We have got to bring people together. But we are a great commonwealth, and we are a great nation, and we are even stronger today because of those actions of those people who came with their bigotry and hatred. I'd now like to introduce the mayor of the city of Charlottesville, Michael Signer.

That might have been the hardest thing I ever did, going up there to speak under those circumstances. I was angry, I was sad, and I was defiant. A fringe element of haters was not going to define us. I believe in people. I believe in humanity. That's true every day, even on as dark a day as that when I was filled with so much sadness. I can't tell you how many people from around the world called or texted to say thank you.

Minyon Moore, whom I'd worked with at the DNC, was on a cruise in the Greek islands with Yolanda Caraway and Leah Daughtry, two of her coauthors on the book *For Colored Girls Who Have Considered Politics*. Charlottesville made news even on their cruise ship, and Minyon started texting me, "Are you OK? Is there anything we can do?"

"I was saying to myself, 'OK, it's already an international story. This is going to be a defining moment for Terry,'" Minyon remembers. "I knew he had to step outside of probably his comfort zone. What happened in Charlottesville was going to get right to the core of who he is as a person. This was important. This could set a tone for America. I think he handled it beautifully. He understood the symbolism of what happened. It's almost like you saw a person grow. A crisis can make you bigger than you should be. He rose to the occasion, and he took his state with him. He was clear that he was not going to sacrifice the values of his state or take the state backward."

It felt like a day that would never end. We left the press conference and drove back to Richmond, where I could visit the families—but first I was going to stop by the mansion to see Sally. Dorothy and I had been worried all afternoon about how Sally and Peter would hear the news about Berke and Jay, so Dorothy reached out to my aide, Jake Rubenstein, who had been with us that morning in Northern Virginia.

"When I got home, Dorothy called me, crying," Jake remembers. "She asked me to go over to the mansion to let Sally know that everything was OK. She was worried that the news was going to report that there was a helicopter crash and Sally would think her father was in there. She didn't want Sally to be alone when she heard that Berke was in the helicopter."

Sally was watching TV when Jake arrived and pulled her away.

"I saw that a state of emergency had been declared and there was some breaking news about an aircraft down," Sally remembers. "That's when I thought through my head, 'My dad went down in a helicopter.'"

Jake assured her that I was fine. He insisted Sally play the basketball game H-O-R-S-E outside with him, and she went along with it, even though it seemed weird to her, since she'd just come back from basketball practice.

"I don't want you to see what's on TV," Jake told her.

"It was a little awkward, because Jake was always funny and kind of a dork, cracking jokes and messing with me," Sally says. "But he was really unsettled. I was like, 'What? When have my parents ever said you can't see what's on CNN?' I thought something was really weird."

Jake did his best to keep her occupied for hours until I was able to get back to the mansion.

"Sally, let's go upstairs and talk," I said.

She followed me up the steps.

"I was really excited to see my dad, because obviously I didn't know what was happening to him all day," Sally says. "But I could tell something was wrong right when he walked through the front door by everyone's faces, especially my dad's."

That was hard, sitting in the armchair where I sat when I told Sally her grandmother had died.

"I know you don't know what's been happening today," I told her. "A helicopter went down and Berke was in it, Berke and Jay."

She stared at me for a minute, her face blank. She was having trouble believing me. Then the truth hit her and she started sobbing. I did my best to comfort her.

"He hugged me for a while, and it was just him and me," Sally says.

I hated to leave her, but I knew I needed to go see the families, and gave her one last hug before I headed back downstairs.

"Marc Wiley knew I had just found out," Sally remembers. "He called me and said, 'Can you please come down to my office?' They comforted me for the remainder of the night. My mom slept with me that night. They knew it would affect me pretty hard."

My next stop after talking to Sally was to see the Cullen family, Jay's wife, Karen, and their two boys, Max and Ryan. We went into the kitchen and it was so hard to make small talk. I tried to talk sports with the boys a little, but no one was in the mood for much talking.

Then we went over to see the Bates family. I paid my condolences to Berke's wife, Amanda, and their eleven-year-old twins, Kylee and Deacon. Those beautiful children, they'd just lost their father. Words felt inadequate. All I could do was show them that I cared, and they knew how much I did. I was crestfallen.

After visiting the families, I'd wanted to stop by the situation room in the Patrick Henry Building to thank everyone for all their hard work that day. We'd all been through such an emotional roller coaster, it was oddly fitting when we sat down together to watch the feed from a drone that was still flying over Charlottesville. We wanted to check to see if, after everything, the situation was stable. We watched the live feed and yes, Kessler and Spencer and their legions were out there somewhere, but at that point they weren't stirring up trouble. All was calm in Charlottesville.

"The city looked really quiet and beautiful at that point," my deputy chief of staff, Suzette Denslow, remembers. "The drone flew all over the city, including the park. I think it gave us a sense of relief that things had settled down and we all hoped it would stay that way."

CHAPTER 9

Sunday, August 13

. . .

Early Sunday morning, we drove from Richmond back to Charlottesville and I went over to John Paul Jones Arena to talk to hundreds of state troopers gathered for their morning briefing. You could hear a pin drop as I walked into the arena. We were all devastated by the loss of Jay and Berke. We'd never find out what exactly happened to Trooper 1, but it was clear it was a catastrophic mechanical failure.

"I was doing some yard work and about to have a beer," an eyewitness, Robert Noll, later told the *Richmond Times-Dispatch*. "There had been helicopters flying over all day, but it made a 'pop, pop, pop' sound like it was missing an engine. . . . It was just above the tree line and it appeared to invert. I just remember it fell tail down."

It was early in the morning, a little after 8 a.m., and it was eerie inside the arena, so quiet. Everyone was in shock. I remember looking out on hundreds of state troopers who had just lost two of their friends, and it was so dimly lit in there you could barely make them out. I talked to them about how Jay had flown me for three and a half years, and Berke had been part of my protection detail for three years until he recently fulfilled a lifelong dream and moved over to the helicopter detail. We all struggled for words that day.

"Today is Berke's forty-first birthday and it just breaks our hearts," I said. "I just spoke to him on Friday."

In conclusion, I said: "I'm devastated for your loss. One of the hardest things as governor is when you lose a member of your State Police. It's like losing part of your family. That's true for Dorothy and me and for our whole family and I know it's true for all of you."

I knew I wasn't going to make any of them feel much better. They were in mourning. But I owed them a show of respect and, given the way I was feeling, there was comfort in sharing my own grief with others who felt the same way about Jay and Berke.

I was also mourning the senseless, heartbreaking death of Heather Heyer. Along with everyone else, I was learning more about her. Her widely circulated post on social media was being cited as a fitting epitaph: "If you're not outraged, you're not paying attention." Heyer had been an activist for years, committed to making a difference, and people were inspired by her example.

"She always had a very strong sense of right and wrong," her mother, Susan Bro, told *HuffPost*. "She always, even as a child, was very caught up in what she believed to be fair. Somehow I almost feel that this is what she was born to be, a focal point for change. I'm proud that what she was doing was peaceful. She wasn't there fighting with people."

One minute Heather was with her friends in quiet, peaceful protest against the neo-Nazis and other white supremacists and in the next minute her life was snatched away. It was just impossible to fathom. As a parent, especially, I felt terrible for Susan Bro and for Heather's father, Mark Heyer. I worked on a statement to send out that day: "My heart goes out to Heather Heyer's family. She died standing up against hate and bigotry. Her bravery should inspire all to come together."

All of the national Sunday TV shows had called to ask me to come on the air that morning, and I had to consider it. I'd been a regular with all of them. As much as I wanted to go on the national shows to express the anger and frustration and outrage that so many of us felt, I decided the time was not right.

This was a morning to focus on the people of Virginia, our pain and our loss. I chose to visit two African American churches that morning, starting at 9:30 at Mount Zion First African Baptist Church, the largest African American church in Charlottesville. I didn't want the day to be about politics. That was why I didn't do any TV. I needed to address Virginians, telling them we needed to come together and move forward. We were going to be stronger because of this.

I led a moment of silence for Berke and Jay and for Heather Heyer, who had all "lost their lives yesterday doing what they loved doing, fighting for freedom and justice."

As I had the day before, I spoke directly to the radical right groups that had converged on Charlottesville from thirty-five different states. I used language that was blunt, direct, and unafraid. There was no reason to be timid or to muddy the waters. You can't fight racism if you don't call out racists. You can't condemn right-wing fanatics if you can't call a Nazi a Nazi and a white supremacist a white supremacist. I could tell my words resonated with the crowd that day in the church.

"Political rhetoric in this country today is breeding bigotry," I said. "We need to call it out for what it is. To the white supremacists and the neo-Nazis who came to our beautiful state yesterday, there is no place for you here in Charlottesville, there is no place for you in Virginia, and there is no place for you in the United

States of America. You pretend you're patriots. You're not patriots. You are a bunch of cowards. I'll tell you this: You only made us stronger. You go home, you stay out of here, because we are a commonwealth that stays together!"

I didn't give a long speech. This was a church service and I didn't want to get in the way.

"What I'm asking you today to do is please put your anger aside, as I did when I got up this morning," I said. "Put it aside. Let us use hope. Let us use today to reach out to our fellow citizens. Let us show these people we are bigger than them. We are stronger than them."

Once I'd finished speaking, I walked down the aisle shaking hands and hugging the parishioners.

"Okay, y'all bring the governor back up here," the pastor, Dr. Alvin Edwards, called out at one point.

I received such a warm reception, he brought me back up. I wanted to start the healing then and there, and this church was the best place to do that.

Jimmy Johnson, who sang in the choir during the day's service, told *The Atlantic*: "Until it's called what it is, just like the governor said, it's going to continue."

I knew many were looking to me to set the right tone, and I wanted to be as positive as I could. You give a lot of speeches in public life, but sometimes it feels like the words just come on their own. Your anger and your hope and your outrage mix together and connect you with your audience in a way that's electric. I love speaking to African American congregations because there's so much excitement, everyone gets very involved, they talk along with you a little, and you know when you're striking a chord.

"Today is a real turning point in our commonwealth of Virginia," I said at the second historically African American church we visited that day, the First Baptist Church, the oldest traditionally African American church in Charlottesville. "Yesterday was a tough day for our state and our beautiful city of Charlottesville. As tough as yesterday was, and it was, this is an opportunity for all of us to show the world who we are. We did have white supremacists, neo-Nazis, come into our beautiful city, carrying semi-automatic weapons, walking up and down our streets. They came here to hurt us, no question about it."

I could hear cries of "Yes!" around the church, urging me on.

"My message is very clear: I not only say, 'Go home,'" I continued. "Get out of the city of Charlottesville. Get out of Virginia. And I would tell you to get out of the United States of America."

"Yes! Yes! Yes!" I could hear.

"You understand nothing of what this country has stood for and fought for. You are haters, you are dividers! So leave this country and never come back."

The applause got so loud, I had to pause.

"I would remind everybody, unless you're Native American," I said, "you're an immigrant from somewhere."

"Amen!" was the answer to that.

"I would remind you that when the first African Americans came to America, they came to Fort Monroe in 1619, and it wasn't their choice to come here to this country! So don't you dare talk to me about white supremacy. What does that even mean, white supremacy? What does that mean? I don't know. I wasn't brought up that way. What does it mean to be a Nazi, where six million members of the Jewish faith were slaughtered? Who are you people? You're not us!"

I'd been carried along by a wave of anger. I felt at home, there in the church, talking to people who I knew shared my outrage.

"You bet I was angry last night," I continued. "But I got up today in a different mind-set. I got up today to say we are going to stand together. We are stronger than these people. You think you hurt us? You didn't hurt us. You made us stronger, ladies and gentlemen. You have emboldened us to fight for every single person who lives in this country, regardless of their race, regardless of their religion."

The applause and affirmations that rang out around the room gave me chills, it was such a strong reaction. It felt like the good people of that congregation and I were taking a journey together that morning.

"To think of these people parading down our streets," I continued. "They used to wear hoods because they were embarrassed. They don't wear hoods anymore. What has brought them to this place in our country?"

I looked around, making eye contact.

"It is a time for healing, it is a time for reconciliation, it is a time for leadership," I said. "I look at this audience and this congregation and I see hope. I see a future that is brighter. I see a future where every single child, no matter where you were born or how you were born or who you love, has the same opportunities as everybody else in our society. That is the United States of America!"

It was such an emotional day. Following the visits to the two churches, I stopped by the UVA medical center to visit as many victims of the violence as I could and to thank the doctors and nurses and everyone at the hospital. Then, this time joined by Dorothy, I visited Jay's family again and visited Berke's family. We had a lot of grief to share.

All around the country that day, "Stand in Solidarity with Charlottesville" rallies and marches were held to mourn Heather Heyer and all the victims of the violence that weekend. The Indivisible Project, which organized events from San Francisco to Washington, DC, urged people to "come together in solidarity with our brave friends in Charlottesville who put themselves at risk to fight against white supremacy," and condemned the hate groups that came to Charlottesville "to push their hateful message of white supremacy, fascism, anti-Semitism, and bigotry."

Also that Sunday, Jason Kessler himself, the organizer of the disastrous "Unite the Right" rally, actually tried to hold a press conference. Can you imagine? His scheming led to three deaths and dozens of injuries, and instead of slinking back into his hole, he was going to do a press conference.

We still had a large Virginia State Police contingent in Charlottesville and sent patrols to ensure this would be a peaceful event with no brawls breaking out. Brian Moran remembers his pride watching State Police march side by side down the Mall to City Hall for the press conference.

"As the unit of troopers marched down the Mall, people who were shopping and enjoying their lunches rose and began applauding," he remembers. "Loud cheers rang out as the troopers made their way toward City Hall. I had successfully kept my emotions in check until that moment. The scene really brought tears to my eyes. After a weekend filled with hate, here was an outpouring of love."

There was no love for Kessler that day. He stepped up to a microphone out in front of City Hall and the crowd that gathered around him yelled so loud, no one could hear a word he said.

"Murderer!" they chanted. "Shame!"

It didn't last long. People converged, some giving him the finger, some screaming at him, and then a woman punched him in the head and he ran off like a scared little child. What a coward.

"I was attacked in front of the whole world, and then people made fun of me for it," Kessler told *The Daily Progress*.

I had no time for his self-pity and lack of self-awareness. I was focused on the work of helping people heal after the trauma of that weekend, and making a fresh start to move beyond the ugliness and hate that Kessler had unleashed.

That afternoon, I joined Levar Stoney—elected Richmond mayor in November 2016—and spiritual leaders at the Slavery Reconciliation Statue in Richmond for a reconciliation rally organized by Richmond State Delegate Delores McQuinn.

"We come today praying for Charlottesville, those who have lost their lives and those who have been hurt," said Delores, who is also a pastor. "We stand in the shadow of this reconciliation statue as a symbolic gesture to remind us that we still have work to do. The battle to fight racism, prejudice, hatred, and the faces of evil is not over. Evil does not just go away without the power, persistence, and prayer of people of goodwill. This is not just the story of a statue in Charlottesville or other places around this nation. It is about what is—and that is evil. That's what it's all about. We battle evil by fighting for the heart and soul of America, democracy, and this nation. We do not fight fire with fire. We fight fire with faith and that's why we are here today."

Levar vowed to do everything he could as mayor to make Richmond inclusive. "There are those who want to take us back to a time of domestic terrorism, of people fearing for their lives," he said. "In this city, in this state, we will not allow that. Collectively, we have to send a message that we will march forward, just like the giants before us."

I got a good round of applause when I spoke out against the alt-right demonstrators who had converged on Charlottesville that weekend and again told them they should "Go home!"

"But let's be honest," I added. "They need to leave America."

I took the opportunity to demand better of the nation's politicians of whatever political party in fighting against racism.

"I call upon every elected official," I said. "We've got to call it out for what it is. It is hatred. It is bigotry. And our leaders have got to be very frank and unequivocal: We will not tolerate that."

We were still on edge that Sunday. The State Police I'd spoken to that morning had remained in Charlottesville. Who knew what else might happen? We thought this invading army of white supremacists might try burning a cross, or worse. We still had a drone in the air that day, looking out for any signs of a disturbance, but it was quiet—and finally, once I got back to the mansion after the reconciliation rally, it was time to send the State Police and National Guard home.

There was a push to have a Sunday night vigil in honor of Heather Heyer, and we could understand how much people wanted to grieve her loss together, but we were very worried that the event could end badly. As it turned out, the event's organizers canceled it, citing a "credible threat from white supremacists."

"On Sunday I was in shock, and almost sleepless, just like everybody," Larry Sabato remembers. Near the Rotunda, he ran into some people who had heard me speak at one of the churches that morning and appreciated my anger because it reflected their own.

"Both downtown and the Rotunda North Plaza had become memorials to those injured and killed," Larry says. "Even Sunday evening was very tense on the Lawn and at the Rotunda. We kept looking in all directions to see whether the Nazis were returning. We watched every tourist with suspicion—which tells you how sick haters can change everyone's perspective."

That Wednesday, at Heather's memorial service, her mother, Susan Bro, gave a moving tribute to her daughter.

"Here's the message," she said. "Although Heather was a caring and compassionate person, so are a lot of you. A lot of you go that extra mile. I think the reason that what happened to Heather has struck a chord is because we know that what she did is achievable. We don't all have to die. We don't all have to sacrifice our lives. They tried to kill my child to shut her up. Well, guess what. You just magnified her."

That led to an amazing moment when the crowd gave her an extended standing ovation.

"I want this to spread," she said. "I don't want this to die. This is just the beginning of Heather's legacy. . . . You make it happen. You take that extra step. You find a way to make a difference in the world."

What a great way to remember her daughter, and Susan Bro was absolutely right: Heather Heyer motivated many people to make a difference.

"She is an inspiration to all of us—to do good, to put a hand out, to help one another," I told reporters after the ceremony.

That night, local activists put together a vigil for Heather in Charlottesville, careful not to put any word of their plans on social media, for fear that white-supremacist agitators would take advantage of the solemn occasion to wreak havoc. In the end the candlelight procession on the Grounds of UVA stretched a quarter mile back from Nameless Field, all the way to the Lawn near the Rotunda. The crowd held a moment of silence for Heather, Berke, and Jay, the three lives lost on Saturday. They were making a powerful statement following the same path of the Friday night torchlight march, replacing tiki torches with candles.

That Friday, we gathered with more than one thousand other mourners at St. Paul's Baptist Church in Richmond to pay our final respects to Berke. Funerals are never easy, but that funeral was one of the tougher ones I've ever been through. We were led into the church by bagpipers, and as we walked in I kept thinking of all the times Berke and I, two proud Irishmen, had celebrated St. Patrick's Day together. The only guy on my EPU unit who requested St. Patrick's Day off every year was Berke. He would get to Rosie Connolly's Pub at ten in the morning; it was just down the hill from the governor's mansion, and he and his buddies would stay there all day. On my first St. Paddy's Day in

Richmond, he suggested I join him for a Guinness at Rosie's, a Shockoe Bottom institution popular with law enforcement, and that became my tradition. I would drive down about 4 o'clock for my annual Guinness toast. And by that time, as my father used to put it, Berke was moving nicely.

The funeral was a painful ordeal for everyone. I think of certain moments from the service that day. The helicopter flyover. The end-of-watch radio call at the end. I still get chills thinking about it.

"He was a character and I'll miss him greatly," I said that day. "I think this is the first time a governor has had to preside over the funeral of a member of his executive protection unit. These individuals live with your family twenty-four hours a day, seven days a week. They're part of our family."

I looked out at the huge assemblage. Berke loved hockey and, as a tribute, dozens of young people he'd coached and players on Kylee and Deacon's team, and friends from his adult league were wearing their hockey jerseys, some over suits and ties. Representatives of law enforcement units gathered from as far away as Alaska, twenty-two states in all, to honor Berke.

I of course told the stories of Jack's care package in Iraq and Sally's first day of high school. Berke was always upbeat and ready to roll. He took his job of protecting us very seriously, but he also always had a little mischief up his sleeve.

That night, after Berke's funeral, we gathered at Rosie Connolly's to pay our respects. Keep in mind, there were troopers there from twenty-two states. The New York State Police delegation came up to me and had a special request.

"We've never met a governor and we've never had a shot with a governor," they said. "Would you help us honor Jay and Berke?"

"Of course!"

That was fine. I was happy to do a shot of Jameson Irish whiskey with the guys from New York. Next thing you know, every other state wanted to do shots with me as well and pose for pictures. What's a governor supposed to do? It was a long night, I'll just leave it at that.

The next day was Jay's funeral. The Cullen family had wanted to hold the services at their Methodist church, but in the end they had to move it to a larger venue, the Southside Church of the Nazarene in nearby Chesterfield county, which could handle the huge throng of more than a thousand people, including hundreds of police officers coming from as far as California and Texas. Colonel Flaherty eulogized Jay, remembering him for his wry smile and wicked sense of humor.

"He listened more than he talked, and when he said something, it was because he had something relevant to say," Flaherty said.

"This is a sad day for our commonwealth," I said. "Jay flew me and my family for the last three and a half years. He took us all over this beautiful commonwealth. . . . He was the most serious, safety-conscious pilot I have ever been with.

"Today we lost a member of our family. Dorothy and I are heartbroken. It will never be the same when I step into that helicopter and not see Jay in the right front seat with 'Cullen' on the back of his helmet. However, when I do get in that helicopter, I will think of Jay, and I will think what a silent giant he was; he was the best of the best of the Virginia State Police."

As the *Richmond Times-Dispatch* reported, "Cullen's funeral was a moving blend of emotion and precision, opening and closing with the moan of bagpipes and snap of snare drums played by officers from Virginia and other states. After seven State Police pallbearers bore Cullen's cremated remains to a gray hearse, Gov. Terry McAuliffe presented a folded Virginia flag to Cullen's widow, Karen, who quietly sobbed. Police helicopters from nine states flew over the church one by one, the thwack-thwack-thwack of their rotors a tribute to Cullen."

CHAPTER 10

Immediate Fallout

. . .

Horrible as it was, Charlottesville did at least show that actions do have consequences. People can be held accountable for their deeds. That's especially true when they congregate in broad daylight and spew some of the ugliest hatred I've ever heard in my life, and assault passive bystanders, all surrounded by hundreds if not thousands of smartphone cameras taking nonstop pictures and videos. Those pictures and videos immediately went up on social media. Alt-right protesters who had lived double lives soon found they could no longer hide from who they really were. They had exposed themselves—and the world took notice, and recoiled. The world shuddered and said, no.

The time in the public eye was especially disastrous for the lead organizer of the "Unite the Right" rally, Jason Kessler. Did his time in the limelight go to his head? Was all that notoriety too much for him? Or was his judgment always seriously suspect? It wasn't enough that he stepped up to that row of microphones to attempt a press conference the day after Heather Heyer, Berke Bates, and

Jay Cullen were killed, and had to turn tail and run. He couldn't help himself.

The following Friday, Kessler went on Twitter and sent out one of the more vile social-media posts I've ever seen: "Heather Heyer was a fat, disgusting Communist. Communists have killed 94 million. Looks like it was payback time."

After that even a lot of Kessler's alt-right fellow travelers wanted nothing to do with him. Richard Spencer, his idol, washed his hands of Kessler. He replied on Twitter, "I will no longer associate w/ Jason Kessler; no one should. Heyer's death was deeply saddening. 'Payback' is a morally reprehensible idea."

Kessler would try various excuses to walk back the despicable attack on Heather, saying he'd taken too much Ambien, suggesting he'd been hacked—but no one seemed to believe any of them. His words were appalling, and they were terrible publicity for the white supremacist movement.

"It's just the exact wrong thing that anyone should be saying at this point, from a moral perspective and from a strategic perspective," Richard Spencer told *The Washington Post*. "This woman did nothing wrong."

Kessler went into hiding, deleting or suspending his various social-media accounts, but the damage had been done. The fish was dying from the head. "Condemnation poured in over the weekend," Kristine Phillips wrote in *The Washington Post*. "The disavowals suggested that the alt-right, a movement that blossomed on social media and the Internet, may be splintering online after the disaster in Charlottesville."

Unfortunately, Charlottesville was the first real opportunity during the Trump administration for these people to act on the license they felt they had from the president of the United States. They felt that they were empowered. Trump's words had unleashed them, launching the scheme of a "Unite the Right" rally, and he had only given them more encouragement when on the day of the tragedy he failed to condemn the neo-Nazis and white supremacists.

Two days later, Trump finally got around to making a clear statement, specifically calling out the KKK and neo-Nazis, as I had on Saturday. "Racism is evil," he said at the White House. "And those who cause violence in its name are criminals and thugs, including the KKK, neo-Nazis, white supremacists, and other hate groups that are repugnant to everything we hold dear as Americans."

No one took his new comments very seriously. The damage was already done. Ken Frazier, CEO of Merck & Co., and two other executives resigned in protest from the American Manufacturing Council over Trump's earlier Charlottesville comments—and were not swayed by the Monday statement.

"The statement today was more 'kumbaya' nonsense," none other than Richard Spencer said on Monday. "He sounded like a Sunday school teacher. I don't think that Donald Trump is a dumb person, and only a dumb person would take those lines seriously."

By the next day, Trump decided to skip the pretext. Talking to reporters at Trump Tower, he said: "I think there is blame on both sides. You had a group on one side that was bad. You had a group on the other side that was also very violent. Nobody wants to say that. I'll say it right now." That was when he added: "You also had some very fine people on both sides."

So much for walking back his earlier racist comments. As *The New York Times* reported, "Venting, his face red as he personally executed the defense of his own actions that no one else would, Mr. Trump all but erased any good will he had earned Monday when he named racist groups and called them 'repugnant to everything we hold dear.'"

David Duke, the KKK leader, loved it—and immediately praised Trump's remarks. A chorus of Republicans denounced

Trump's "very fine people on both sides" retreat from his words a day earlier. Trump economic adviser Gary Cohn drafted a resignation letter after standing in the lobby of Trump Tower during the president's outburst, but ultimately delayed his exit from the administration until March 2018.

The combination of the Charlottesville tragedy and Trump's insistence on further inflaming both his supporters and critics came across almost as a challenge, and many responded. These guys thought they were going to have themselves a wild weekend, going out and kicking some ass and having some fun, splitting some heads, beating some people up, men or women, they didn't care. Never for a second did they stop to think they could lose their jobs over it. Their faces were put up on social media, and then they were hounded.

Logan Smith of Raleigh, North Carolina, started a Twitter account, @YesYoureRacist, and started posting pictures and videos of torch-carrying white supremacists. One of the first the site focused on—and named—was Cole White, a twenty-three-year-old who traveled all the way from the San Francisco Bay Area to Charlottesville specifically with the intent of wreaking havoc. Soon after Smith posted White's picture at the Friday-night torch rally at UVA, he lost his job at Top Dog, a famous Berkeley hot-dog joint one block from campus known for libertarian politics, over the public outcry.

By December 2018, White was pleading guilty in U.S. district court to federal charges stemming from his violent actions in Charlottesville. Law enforcement did great work. They had White and he knew it, so in court he confirmed the obvious, that he flew to Virginia in August 2017 specifically to "engage in violent confrontations with protesters or other individuals at the upcoming events in Charlottesville."

A spokesman for the U.S. attorney's office offered this explanation of White's actions at the Friday-night march: "Violence erupted among the crowd, with some individuals punching, kicking, spraying chemical irritants, swinging torches, and otherwise assaulting others, all resulting in a riot. Among that riot, White admitted today to swinging his torch and striking several individuals and that none of these acts of violence was taken in self-defense."

At the "Unite the Right" rally the next day, White and other members of the Rise Above Movement (RAM) moved into a group of counterprotesters and "collectively punched, pushed, kicked, choked, head-butted, and otherwise assaulted several individuals resulting in a riot. White admitted to personally committing multiple acts of violence. For example, after having already made his way through a group, White turned around and observed a protester blocking the sidewalk by holding on to a street sign. White walked back, grabbed the individual by the shoulders, and punched him until he released the sign. White then head-butted a male whom he perceived was in his way. Finally, White head-butted a female protester who was present on the sidewalk, resulting in a laceration to her face."

Part of the horror of that weekend was how brazen these racists were. It was unbelievable that weekend to see so many young men showing their faces and engaging in such vile acts. They didn't cover their faces, even though they knew they were being photographed, and seemed to welcome the attention. One by one, many of them joined Cole White in regretting that they could ever have been so un-American.

A. C. Thompson reported in his *Frontline* documentary "Documenting Hate: Charlottesville" on Vasilios Pistolis, an active duty United States Marine Corps Lance Corporal. Thompson was able to identify Pistolis as a neo-Nazi participant in the Charlottesville violence, active in hard-core neo-Fascist groups like the Atomwaffen Division and Traditionalist Worker Party—and made him pay a price.

I'm the proud son of an Army captain and the proud father of a Marine captain, and it was shocking to hear that a United States Marine lance corporal could be capable of such hateful violence. "Today cracked three skulls open with virtually no damage to myself," Pistolis posted online the day of the "Unite the Right" rally. "Photographs taken at the rally show Pistolis clubbing an unidentified counter-protester with a wooden flagpole," Thompson wrote. "Pistolis would later post photos of his bloody custom-made Confederate flag to chat logs, with the addendum, 'not my blood.' Pistolis also bragged about assaulting a well-known local activist, Emily Gorcenski, on the night of August 11, 2017. Multiple videos taken that evening show Pistolis, dressed in a black Adidas tracksuit, launch a flying kick in the direction of Gorcenski, although it is unclear if he connected. In Atomwaffen's chats, Pistolis claimed that 'I drop kicked Emily Gorcenski.'"

On August 1, 2018, a Marine spokesman announced that Pistolis, after having been court-martialed and spending a month in the brig at Camp Lejeune, North Carolina, had "officially been separated from the Marine Corps."

Justice had also come for men who had severely beaten De-Andre Harris, a twenty-year-old African American, in a parking garage in Charlottesville the afternoon of the "Unite the Right" rally. One of the four found guilty, fifty-year-old Tyler Watkins Davis of Florida, "was seen on video whacking Harris on the head with a wooden stick—a tire thumper," prosecutors told Judge Richard E. Moore. "The injury gave Harris such a large laceration on his head that it required eight staples."

The verdicts against some of the worst violent offenders in

Charlottesville made international headlines. "Video of the garage attack—and of Harris's bloodied head—sped across the Internet, ultimately helping online sleuths, led by journalist Shaun King, to identify the assailants," Ian Shapiro wrote in the London *Independent*. "The three others are: Jacob S. Goodwin, twenty-four, a white nationalist from Arkansas who received an eight-year sentence; Alex Michael Ramos, of Georgia, who got six years; and Daniel Borden, of Ohio, who is serving a nearly four-year sentence. . . . Video evidence showed that by the time Harris was fully in the garage, he was scrambling on the floor and the assailants—armed with a shield, a wooden board or a stick—were standing over him in a full-scale attack."

Probably the highest-profile conviction was of James Alex Fields, the neo-Nazi terrorist who revved up his muscle car and drove into the crowd of peaceful protesters that Saturday afternoon, murdering Heather Heyer in cold blood and injuring dozens of others. In December 2018, a jury released its verdict, finding Fields guilty and recommending that he be sentenced to 419 years in prison and given $480,000 in fines. Fields's lawyers tried to claim that he was acting in self-defense when he drove his Dodge Challenger down the narrow street crowded with defenseless people, but the jury had no trouble rejecting that defense as absurd.

"This trial and today's outcome has been a long time coming for the victims and their family members," the chief prosecutor in the case, Joe Platania, said after the jury verdict was announced. "We are unable to heal their physical injuries or bring Heather back. But we are hopeful they'll be able to take some comfort and solace from these verdicts and sentences."

Susan Bro, Heather's mother, also spoke after the verdict. "So many emotions, so many reactions, it's really still hard to process," she said. "So we move forward. We still have social justice work to do."

Talking to me for this book, Susan questioned the preparedness on the ground in Charlottesville; for example, the wooden sawhorse that was placed down in an attempt to block off Fourth Street. "The fact that they knew how to block off the street when she already had been killed and knew how to put up permanent barriers for a month tells me they knew how to do it in the first place, they just didn't do it," she said.

But she also told me it does no good to blame anyone. "The bottom line is, human beings were in that situation, and I don't think any of us are completely responsible for him driving his car into that crowd," she said. "We all maybe would have done things differently had we known. But, bottom dollar, he chose to put his foot on that gas pedal. He was sitting at the top of the hill as they started up Fourth Street, I saw in the police evidence. He was already sitting there. He had already pulled down and backed up and decided he would make that choice after they came up the street. So I certainly don't hold Charlottesville police responsible for that. That's just what happened."

A lawsuit filed by the nonprofit Integrity First for America on behalf of ten Charlottesville plaintiffs, some injured in James Fields's terrorist car attack, was moving forward in the courts in early 2019 with a trial set for July. The case, filed under the Ku Klux Klan Act of 1871, targeted twenty-five prominent white supremacists, including Jason Kessler and James Fields, and—as the group's website explains—"Richard Spencer, a white nationalist who believes in 'ethnic cleansing,' [and] Matthew Heimbach, a white nationalist who said, 'Of course we look up to men like Adolf Hitler.'"

Ku Klux Klan leader Richard Preston, a self-professed KKK imperial wizard in Maryland, pleaded no contest to firing his handgun at the rally in Charlottesville—and was sentenced to four years in prison. He'd founded a group called the Confederate White Knights of the KKK, but later tried to claim he was not a racist and was only in Charlottesville to keep the peace.

Just to underscore how the alt-right unraveled and opened itself up to mockery in the aftermath of Charlottesville, the "Crying Nazi," Christopher Cantwell, responded to the Fields jury decision with a flurry of hateful gibberish, something about how the verdict was going to inspire the "complete and total destruction" of the "broad Left."

Cantwell was barred from setting foot in the commonwealth of Virginia for five years after pleading guilty to two counts of assault and battery for his hooliganism in Charlottesville. He appeared in a video on Vox that soon turned viral.

"None of the marchers soared so high or crashed so hard as Chris Cantwell, who became the ivory-skinned, gun-toting star of a documentary about Charlottesville that aired Monday on HBO—and a week later is better known as the 'weeping Nazi' who got banned from OkCupid," *The Washington Post* reported.

"'I've been told there's a warrant out for my arrest,' Cantwell pleads to the camera, through sniffles and a trembling voice. 'I don't know what to do!'" *The Post* reported.

Charlottesville police had reportedly issued felony warrants for his arrest on charges of "illegal use of gases" and "injury by caustic agent or explosive."

"In his confessional, Cantwell told the camera he was too scared to go to the courthouse or meet police," *The Post* continued. "He complained that Chelsea Manning had been threatening to 'curb-stomp Nazis.' . . . 'I know we talk a lot of s— on the Internet,' Cantwell said. But: 'Every step of the way we've tried to do the right thing and they just won't stop.'"

These crybabies and cowards had to learn the hard way that you're responsible for your actions—and you will pay a price.

Word started reaching us that Jason Kessler was trying to organize a "Unite the Right 2" rally in Charlottesville for August 2018, one year later. He was actually hoping to go big and organize two rallies that month, one in Charlottesville and one in Washington, DC. The Charlottesville plans never panned out. Charlottesville denied his request for a permit on the grounds that the rally he wanted to organize would inevitably turn violent. Kessler applied for a permit to stage a protest in Lafayette Square in Washington, DC, and it was approved. The event itself fizzled, with only a couple of dozen protesters showing up.

Once again, it was the video making the rounds afterward that everyone remembered, as Vox reported—under the headline THE ORGANIZER OF THE CHARLOTTESVILLE RALLY JUST GOT HUMILIATED BY HIS OWN FATHER—in a piece by Zack Beauchamp.

"It was a dreary failure," Beauchamp reported from the protest. "I walked around the crowd of counterprotesters that dwarfed the neo-Nazis by orders of magnitude. But as pathetic as all of that was, none of it was quite as hilariously humiliating to the alt-right as the video below—in which the rally's organizer, Jason Kessler, is yelled at by his father to get out of his parents' room in the middle of a live stream with a fellow alt-righter. . . . Kessler says, in the livestream, that he has been forced to move in with his parents after a series of lawsuits stemming from last year's violence sapped his funds. It's an arrangement neither he nor his father seems pleased about. 'Hey!' Kessler's father says, '. . . You get out of my room!'"

Boy, how the mighty have fallen. Beauchamp's conclusion: "The alt-right movement—which supporters hoped and analysts feared would become stronger and more mainstream after Charlottesville—has actually devolved into farce, with one of its key figures literally living at his parents' house and sneaking into his father's room to film his hateful videos."

The alt-right movement was in disarray, with so many of its leaders in jail, sniping at each other, or leaving the movement—but its notoriety still had a toxic influence. Robert Bowers, the white nationalist who murdered eleven people at the Tree of Life Synagogue in Pittsburgh, was apparently egged on by some mix of anger over Charlottesville participants being held to account and online conspiracy theories about the alleged "caravan" of Central Americans heading toward the United States.

"For some, though, Charlottesville served to harden their resolve, to push them deeper into white supremacist ideology," A. C. Thompson told me. "After Charlottesville, a lot of these younger guys—and they're overwhelmingly guys—turned toward terrorism. They said, 'Rallies don't work, political parties don't work, Trump isn't doing what we want. The only answer is terrorism.' They began idolizing guys like Timothy McVeigh, the Oklahoma City bomber; and Dylann Roof, who shot up the African American church in Charleston, South Carolina; and Anders Breivik, a Norwegian man who killed seventy-seven people, many of them children. This faction of the white supremacist movement is stockpiling weapons and explosives. They want to set off [a] race war and topple the government. These are the kind of people I worry about now. You don't need a lot of money or a lot of technical sophistication to commit a mass-scale act of violence. Look at Robert Bowers, the man accused of murdering eleven Jewish congregants at the Tree of Life Synagogue in Pittsburgh. It seems Bowers was part of this new terrorist milieu."

CHAPTER 11

Practical Lessons Learned

■ ■ ■

All we talked about in the weeks after Charlottesville was how we could take the pain and anger we all felt and turn it into a positive. What could be learned? What changes could be made to help avoid ever witnessing such a terrible spectacle in our streets again? The Nazis and white supremacists who had descended on Charlottesville might have left town, but they wouldn't be easily forgotten. That display of hatred would be seared into the minds of Americans for years to come. I called an emergency cabinet meeting on the Monday morning just after Charlottesville. I was well aware that no government commissions were ever going to offer all the answers, but they could sure move the discussion forward.

We needed to focus on a racist and anti-Semitic subculture that was clearly finding a way to thrive in America, whether some cared to admit it or not. Next, we needed to take every step possible to make sure that level of violence never again occurred in Virginia, or anywhere else. I knew without a doubt that we'd done everything we could at the state level to prepare for Charlottesville, but obviously somewhere in the implementation and coordination those plans went off the rails. Our bitter experience left Virginia well poised to serve as a leader for other states facing similar protests.

In fact, Charlie Baker, the Republican governor of Massachusetts, called me that Monday to offer his solidarity and to express his outrage over what happened in Charlottesville, but mostly he wanted my advice. They had a huge rally coming up in Boston.

"Charlie, you've got to get control of your permit process," I told him. "The key to controlling this type of protest is to keep the two sides separated. Build in a buffer zone."

At our cabinet meeting that Monday morning, I turned to Brian Moran.

"Brian, what's our plan?" I said.

"Governor, we need to launch an After-Action Review [AAR] to assess what went well and what didn't, and clearly identify areas of improvement," he said. "We also need to look into permitting processes at the state and local level."

"Good, let's get to work."

We all knew we had to address the permitting issue. Charlottesville authorities had boxed themselves into a corner and let Jason Kessler's permit be approved automatically, with no restrictions whatsoever. That should never have been allowed to happen. Next time would have to be different.

This was no theoretical exercise. The Sunday *Richmond Times-Dispatch* had just published a story reporting that "a Confederate heritage organization has asked the state for permission to gather September 16 at Richmond's Robert E. Lee monument." There were also reports that another group, Save Southern Heritage, was seeking a permit to rally on the same day at the same monument. We knew that once these groups started organizing, others would get the word and come out of the woodwork.

How would we respond? The permit as it existed would have

allowed up to five thousand people. There was zero chance that five thousand people could fit into this roundabout in the middle of downtown Richmond. Five hundred, maybe, if we stacked people on top of each other. There was no way I was going to let this stand.

Since the monument was on state property, as governor I had jurisdiction, and signed Executive Order 67, which temporarily suspended permitting at the Lee Monument in Richmond for ninety days, pending a thorough review. "State and local officials need to get ahead of this problem, so that we have the proper legal protections in place to allow for peaceful demonstrations, but without putting citizens and property at risk," I explained that day. "Let me be clear, this executive order has nothing to do with infringing upon First Amendment rights. This is a temporary suspension, issued with the singular purpose of creating failsafe regulations to preserve the health and well-being of our citizens and ensuring that nothing like what occurred in Charlottesville happens again."

And can you believe it? The ACLU promptly complained, calling my executive order "constitutionally suspect." Once again, it was the executive director of the ACLU of Virginia. I figured it wouldn't be long until the ACLU sued us over suspending protests, and I welcomed their challenge.

"It is a sad reality of this moment that nearly every protest carries with it a risk of violence," she said in a statement. "Protecting the First Amendment in the current context requires extremely careful and thoughtful decision-making by the government officials in whom we place our trust. We cannot allow fear and loathing to drive us to abdicate the rule of law or temper our fealty to basic constitutional principles. We cannot allow government to use safety considerations as a thin veil for broad and sweeping prior restraints on our speech or other expressive activities in public spaces.

"We must require our leaders to follow accepted case law that requires a finding by a judge that any proposed prior restraint on speech is justified by concrete evidence of an imminent threat of harm by a particular speaker or speakers. The decisions we allow our leaders to make in this moment should not be ones that empower future leaders to use them as precedent in the pursuit of tyranny. Without a safe, secure, and nonviolent space for the free expression of ideas—even the most hateful ones—there can be no true freedom in academic, artistic, scientific, or political affairs."

This was an absurd argument against a temporary suspension until the permitting process could be reviewed and revised. However, in a sign that the ACLU may have learned from its mistakes, it made no move in court against the executive order. I think they had finally realized how badly they had mishandled Charlottesville.

Nationally, the Virginia ACLU's handling of the Charlottesville crisis had a lot of people very uncomfortable. On August 12, Waldo Jaquith had tweeted out: "I just resigned from the ACLU of Virginia board. What's legal and what's right are sometimes different. I won't be a fig leaf for Nazis."

"This was a real tragedy and we're all reeling," Lee Rowland, an ACLU attorney in New York, told the Associated Press that month. "Charlottesville should be a wake-up call to all of us."

K-Sue Park, a UCLA law professor, weighed in with a *New York Times* op-ed headlined THE ACLU NEED TO RETHINK FREE SPEECH. "By insisting on a narrow reading of the First Amendment, the organization provides free legal support to hate-based causes," Park wrote. "The ACLU needs a more contextual, creative advocacy when it comes to how it defends the freedom of speech. The group should imagine a holistic picture of how speech rights are under attack right now, not focus on only First Amendment case law. . . . Sometimes standing on the wrong side of history in defense of a cause you think is right is still just standing on the wrong side of history."

We started brainstorming other ideas for how to address the broader cultural issues. What had changed to bring these racists out into the light of day? How could young white men wearing swastikas feel so unashamed and even proud marching with torches? How could they march down a city street screaming the f-ing n-word?

"The rally reflected a shift in the swastika's place in the iconography of American hate," Rick Hampson wrote in *USA Today*. "It is more popular than ever among non-ideological haters—kids, vandals, anyone out to shock or rebel or express a personal grudge against someone who happens to be Jewish, black, Hispanic or gay."

America's eyes were on Virginia and we needed bold action. This was an opportunity for Virginia to lead the way. I also signed two other executive orders. The first, EO 68, directed Brian Moran to establish a Task Force on Public Safety Preparedness and Response to Civil Unrest. The second, EO 69, created a Commonwealth Commission on Diversity, Equity, and Inclusion, "to identify policy changes that can be made at the state level to combat intolerance, expand opportunity for all, and make Virginia more open and inclusive to people from every walk of life."

As cochairs of the Diversity Commission I selected Rabbi Jack Moline, executive director of Interfaith Alliance, who had been recognized by *Newsweek* magazine as one of the most influential rabbis in the country, and Cynthia Hudson, Virginia's chief deputy attorney general, a former labor lawyer and law professor at the College of William and Mary who was also a city attorney in Hampton, Virginia, for eight years.

"In the wake of the tragic events in Charlottesville, it is important for the people of Virginia to have an honest discussion about what we can do to combat hatred and violence and continue our work building a commonwealth that is open and welcoming to everyone," I said at the time. "The white supremacists and Klansmen who descended upon Charlottesville do not represent the values of the vast majority of Virginians, and the problems of white supremacy, religious intolerance, discrimination against LGBT Virginians, and other forms of hatred and violence are not unique to this commonwealth. But those events should be a wakeup call for every citizen about the need to work together constructively to examine the origins of racism, discrimination, and radicalization, and what steps we can take to drive those pernicious forces from our commonwealth and our country."

Traci DeShazor, our deputy secretary of the commonwealth, headed up our effort to put a broad and diverse commission together. We named thirty-two individuals to the commission, from Hassan Ahmad, an immigration lawyer from Sterling, Virginia, to Jonathan Zur of Richmond, president and CEO of the Virginia Center for Inclusive Communities. We had a vibrant mix of office holders, professors, advocacy groups, and others—and a lot of ground to cover, to say the least. "One of the challenges was, we realized just how large this conversation could be and how many directions it could go," Traci recalled.

The commission's work continues, as of March 2019, when I was putting this book to bed, but I look forward to its final report. One point they've made is that you never start too soon when it comes to issues of diversity and acceptance, which need to be included in our schools' curriculums. We need to find ways to educate our children about racism and intolerance at an early age. It starts at home, but from the time children first start school, we need to reinforce a healthy regard for respecting the dignity of all.

You have to be very serious about combatting the scourge of virulent racism in all its insidious and subtle forms. A lot of the people who end up as white supremacists had an early start. These ideas and prejudices are typically ingrained in them when they are very young. That's why it's so critical to focus on more diversity and more inclusion from the time children are just starting out in school, so from the outset that's what they know and what they expect.

I wanted the Task Force on Public Safety Preparedness and Response to Civil Unrest to consider the results of the AAR, take a hard look at our preparations and response, and develop a set of permitting guidelines for use by state and local authorities.

Brian, Curtis, and Nicky started the process of hiring an outside firm to provide staff support to the task force and conduct the AAR. Our work on permitting had to be prioritized first in order to get the regulations in place for the Lee monument in Richmond. Before long we had a team of contractors researching what other states and localities were doing with regard to incidents of hate-group rallies and demonstrations and permitting. It was clear that these types of events were becoming more prevalent, and they were here to stay. Shockingly, though, we quickly learned that there weren't any clear best practices out there.

Most localities assumed that the First Amendment prevented them from developing restrictive permitting processes. But in fact, if you can persuasively articulate a credible public-safety risk, then the First Amendment still affords you the latitude to impose certain reasonable restrictions, for example on the time and place of protest. You can balance public safety issues, provided you can articulate the reasons for the restrictions and they are clearly not based on the content of the speech. In Charlottesville, authorities should have clearly stated that there were going to be a thousand white supremacists, many of them armed and dangerous and attending with the explicit intent of inciting violence, and likely double that number in counterprotesters. They couldn't provide safety to that number of people.

Brian had also hired Shannon Dion, a lawyer from the Department of Criminal Justice Services, to help with the constitutional research around permitting. She remembered one of her law professors from the University of Richmond, Rodney Smolla, a First Amendment scholar. He had even defended three guys who had been convicted for burning a cross in someone's front yard, arguing that it was an act of free speech. I didn't love his position on the cross-burning, but I knew that if anyone could advise us on this topic, he was the man.

Smolla, now the dean at the Widener School of Law at the University of Delaware, gladly dug into this project and had a team of law students researching the issue. He confirmed that we could absolutely have a strong permitting process, and with his guidance, we developed a process that made sense for Richmond's Lee monument and for other localities to use. We learned later that Smolla had been called on to advise the U.S. Supreme Court on First Amendment issues as they related to permitting.

We had hired a respected outside group, the International Association of Chiefs of Police, to conduct the AAR. When it was finalized in November, we had a better idea of what had happened. They presented the task force with a number of issues that needed to be addressed, and they adopted several recommendations to present to me.

The AAR report concluded—in big red type—"Recommendations communicated by the state to the City of Charlottesville were not accepted, including industry best practices for handling violent events."

Looking forward, the report emphasized the following recommendations:

- Agencies should adhere to the National Incident Management System (NIMS) and Incident Command standards, including joint training

- Maximize use of related state assets and resources
- Inter-governmental and community coordination

Given the global reach of social media, online chat rooms, and the rest, the game had been changed. These thugs had successfully recruited fellow thugs from thirty-five states across the country using social media. They were basically a bunch of professional protesters and their goal was to come in, incite violence, and create chaos. We knew we were up against some bad actors. Their network was deep and widespread.

We learned after the fact that there was confusion about the operational plan. There hadn't been consensus on a single incident action plan, which meant that all of our people weren't on the same page. That's why the incident management team was so critical. The IMT is a multi-disciplinary team, so they know how to integrate all of the different players into one plan and make sure that everyone has the right version. NIMS also makes sure that everyone is properly coordinated from an operations and decision-making standpoint. To really get this moving, we would need training. I ended up providing about $1 million to hold statewide training.

The International Association of Chiefs of Police credited Virginia state authorities with "thorough preparation" ahead of the "Unite the Right" rally and determined that we had provided "ample resources" to Charlottesville.

"Without the presence of such a large, well-trained, well-equipped contingent of state assets," the report concluded, "arguably the outcome of the event could have been far worse. . . . During interviews, city officials spoke very highly of the support they received from the Commonwealth, in particular from the Virginia State Police."

We knew what worked. We'd established that in September when a planned pro-Confederate rally at the Lee statue in Richmond prompted me to issue the executive order putting a ninety-day moratorium on any permits for the Lee statue. However, a few diehards decided to come to Richmond from out of state anyway, and stand on the sidewalk across the street from the Lee statue.

Our team worked closely with Mayor Stoney and Richmond Chief of Police Alfred Durham, and they took all the basic precautions we wanted to institute before Charlottesville, including banning knives, poles, sticks, and masks at the gathering. They also had an effective plan to keep the alt-right marchers separated from any counterprotesters. The result? Success. Violence was avoided. There was no trouble.

It showed that even when dangerous racists come in from out of state, an event can be kept under control. The *Richmond Times-Dispatch* talked to twenty-year-old white supremacist Erik Pulley, who said he was there from Wilson, North Carolina. "I was born and raised, you know, in the KKK, Aryan Brotherhood," he told the *Times-Dispatch*. "I believe in supporting these monuments, because you never see a black person—a black monument being torn down, do you?"

But the good news was, Pulley was joined by only half a dozen other like-minded individuals.

"About seven people stood for an hour and a half holding Confederate flags and arguing with a crowd of counterprotesters that steadily climbed into the hundreds until police ushered the Confederates away," the *Times-Dispatch* reported. It all would have gone very smoothly if not for a small mishap. Rally organizers headed back to their truck only to find they had two flat tires—making it hard for them to flee. "A crowd of several dozen counterprotesters confronted and then chased them as they attempted to drive away in the disabled vehicle," the *RTD* added. "The group made it several blocks through the Fan District before stopping and waiting with police for a tow truck."

CHAPTER 12

Rallying Cry

. . .

One of the first things Dorothy and I did after I was inaugurated as governor of Virginia in January 2014 was to make a few changes at the governor's mansion in Richmond. When we walked in, we walked from room to room and everywhere you looked there were paintings of old white men. There were no portraits of African Americans displayed on the walls of the mansion. Not one. We changed that.

Dorothy and I decided that the first piece of art we'd put up would be a portrait of an unnamed African American working man painted by Pierre Daura, a Catalan artist who fought in the Spanish Civil War before relocating to Virginia with his American wife. The portrait, lent to us by the Library of Virginia, is of a custodian at Randolph–Macon Women's College in Lynchburg, Virginia, where Daura taught in the late 1940s. We were proud to honor that working man as a symbol of so many other working people who were not being celebrated, but we knew it was only a start.

We also wanted to honor Oliver Hill, the great African American civil rights lawyer from Richmond whose work was a critical part of the *Brown v. Board of Education* case before the United States Supreme Court in the 1950s. Hill lived to be one hundred. On Juneteenth in 2015 we had a ceremony at the governor's mansion to unveil a portrait of Hill that we displayed in the front room right next to Patrick Henry's desk. Our mansion director, Kaci Easley, arranged for the painting to be loaned from the University of Richmond Black Law Students Association. We had more than one hundred guests for the occasion, including Hill's son, Dr. Oliver W. Hill Jr., a psychology professor at Virginia State University.

"Mr. Hill was a trailblazer like no other," I said at the ceremony.

Next we located a portrait to borrow from the historic Robert Russa Moton Museum of remarkable leader Barbara Johns, who in April 1951 led the famous Moton High School walkout in Farmville, Virginia. That walkout ultimately became part of the *Brown v. Board of Education* case. She was sixteen years old at the time. Imagine the courage! She could have been lynched for gathering the students, more than four hundred of them, in the school gymnasium and marching them to the local courthouse to protest segregation and the overcrowding and dilapidated conditions of her blacks-only school. That courage helped lead to the Supreme Court's decision on *Brown v. Board of Education* overturning state-sponsored segregation of public schools. And after the verdict, you know what they did in Farmville? They shut down all the schools for six years rather than integrating their schools under Supreme Court order. That was one of the worst things done in the history of the commonwealth, literally offering no education to these students.

We had a ceremony at the mansion to honor Barbara Johns and invited sister, brothers, children, and grandchildren to attend. It was a celebration of a remarkable person, but it was also a celebration of telling the full story of Virginia and the United

States. And from that day on her portrait has been displayed in the ballroom where all official receptions at the mansion are held.

I thought of those portraits and the larger story they told in the aftermath of the Charlottesville tragedy. That horrible weekend shook up the country. It held up a mirror and showed us a picture of America that caused many of us to recoil. It may have been only a fringe element showing up in the streets of Charlottesville, but they were marching in broad daylight, seemingly unashamed of having such a twisted view of humanity and acting out, often with savage violence.

It's not as if we're going to turn the pain of Charlottesville into instant and obvious progress. Maybe we're past the point of believing in progress as anything other than an awkward, slow succession of advances and setbacks, but that only means we redouble our efforts and keep fighting for progress. Breakthroughs do happen. Surprises do come.

I don't think I've met a more inspirational figure in my life than the South African leader Nelson Mandela, imprisoned all those years on Robben Island, who emerged with no bitterness and led his people to freedom after years of apartheid. I visited him in South Africa on his ninetieth birthday and he reiterated to me his famous quote: "No one is born hating another person because of the color of his skin, or his background, or his religion. People must learn to hate, and if they can learn to hate, they can be taught to love, for love comes more naturally to the human heart than its opposite."

But Mandela was not only eloquent on racism and hate, he was also wise about understanding the lure of vanity and its dangers, especially for any man or woman who would lead. "As I have said, the first thing is to be honest with yourself," he said. "You can never have an impact on society if you have not changed yourself. . . . Great peacemakers are all people of integrity, of honesty, but humility."

Charlottesville was a reminder that we need to keep embracing change, not for show but as a daily, constant progression. Too often when it comes to racism and its twisted and disfiguring legacy, we as a country have been almost like a New Year's Day resolution–maker, waking up from a deep sleep, hungover, shocked to fathom what our past has held, vowing to make a show of being different. That's a form of vanity, repeating the same cycle over and over, discovery and remedy, discovery and remedy.

Let's have fewer promises. Let's make fewer resolutions. Let's do less posturing. Note to all of us white people: We're never going to know what it's like to grow up black in a country with a racist past and a present where racism holds sway far too often. We're never going to fully understand what it's like to be a person of color in a racist society. We're never going to move forward unless we acknowledge that institutional racism exists. I believe that if we work together we can move beyond our racist past.

The midterm elections of 2018 represented a historic wave. It started in 2017 in Virginia when we picked up the most House of Delegate seats in more than 140 years, and a historic number of them were women. In 2018, more women were elected to the U.S. Congress than ever before, more people volunteered and canvassed to encourage people to vote than ever before in an off-year election, and the newly elected congress arrived in Washington as part of a young, talented, and resourceful group committed to bringing change. I love to see the fresh energy and fresh ideas. I love that faith in the human capacity to bring progress, because that's the spark at the heart of democracy. I believe in what government can do to promote and protect the common good if we come together, put our biases aside, and focus on bettering the lives of each and every American.

Our democracy is what we make of it. The Charlottesville tragedy, like so much of the Trump years, was about certain individuals clinging to the past, and not wanting to move beyond a familiar, often false, picture of how things used to be. Some of the white supremacists who converged on Virginia that weekend later recanted and claimed they were no longer alt-right extremists. We have reason to be skeptical of those claims—but maybe in some cases there were individuals who saw what a dead end that was. Or others who were turned off by leaders like Jason Kessler, getting yelled at by his dad in the middle of trying to peddle propaganda about his glorious vision of white supremacist vengeance. In the end, Charlottesville was the worst thing that ever happened to these groups. As I predicted on August 12, they emerged fractured and weakened, and Virginia came out stronger.

Our best defense against extremists and preachers of hate is to get to work on the changes we know are badly overdue. That's how you bring about progress, moving forward together on so many fronts, from education and health care to good-paying jobs.

I asked State Senator Lionell Spruill Sr. what he saw as the top priorities for the African American community and he replied, "Schools, health care, and criminal justice reform. We need to continue the work that you started with juvenile justice reform and facilities, and put that back on the front burner."

We have to educate young people about racism and bigotry, and we have to prepare students from all backgrounds to have real opportunities. A lot of children from broken homes get in trouble early on, and in the past once they entered the system, that tended to define their futures. But we can't throw away the key on a kid who got in trouble. Too often that's what happens.

Early in my time as governor, we had way too many juveniles in the facilities overseen by the Virginia Department of Juvenile Justice (DJJ), which were in many cases obsolescent or borderline obsolescent. The whole program was badly in need of some fresh thinking and fresh energy. In 2014, I recruited as DJJ director a national leader on youth advocacy, Andrew K. Block Jr., who was then director of the UVA School of Law Child Advocacy Clinic. During my term, we were able to reduce the juvenile correctional population by 68 percent.

At the start of my administration there were two large, outmoded facilities, the Beaumont Juvenile Correctional Center in Powhatan County and the Bon Air Juvenile Correctional Center in Chesterfield County. You'd have thought you were going to a maximum-security prison, getting a look at these gigantic concrete structures, which makes sense, since in fact both facilities were built for the purpose of incarcerating adults. It was an outrage to have juveniles locked in these adult prisons with little hope or opportunity.

I sat down for a meeting with a group of fourteen-, fifteen-and sixteen-year-olds gathered around a table. Some of them were slouching, all of them looked distracted. As Andy Block remembers, "Some of these kids had no idea who a governor was or what he did."

But I was there to listen and I did my best to get them talking.

"What can we do at the state level to help you?" I asked.

They looked skeptical. Finally one young man spoke up.

"You say you want to help," he said. "How can we learn if we don't have internet access?"

It was a fair point. Some of these young people were in these facilities for serious offenses, but many of them just needed to find a path forward in life. Getting them access to online educational courses made sense.

On the way home, I called my secretary of technology, Karen Jackson.

"You have sixty days to get Wi-Fi in both facilities," I told her.

They got their Wi-Fi. Reaching these young people was not that complicated. You needed to treat them like individuals, and show you cared, not process them like cogs in a giant factory. We decided to shut down these large, outmoded facilities, starting with Beaumont, and move as many of these kids as we could to smaller, treatment-based facilities, which offered more counseling and were closer to their families. The staff at these facilities was dedicated and effective, but they just didn't have the resources to do what they needed to do.

We saved money through our reforms and allocated more of that for treatment programs, so kids in rural areas might have access to the same programs as kids in larger metropolitan areas. Some of the savings was also spent upgrading Bon Air, both its programs and facilities. Under Andy Block's leadership, reforms were instituted across the board based on knowledge of what really works.

As Dave Ress of the *Daily Press* in Newport News reported in a January 2019 article, "Staff members don't wear the old metal law enforcement badges they used to, and the men and women who were once called correctional officers are now called residential supervisors or community coordinators. They are stationed in the housing units, and they stay with the same group, rather than rotating as they used to do. They've had training in counseling, particularly focused on helping youth deal with trauma, which recent studies suggest is a key factor when young people get into trouble."

The article reported that the reforms we launched had led to a 90 percent reduction in "aggressive incidents" at state facilities.

"We used to see fights every day," Sage Williams, a nineteen-year-old at Bon Air, told the reporter. "Now, maybe it's a couple a week. It just feels a lot safer now."

We supported programs at Bon Air like a student government

association, a nine-month in-house barber school, and a quilting and upholstering program, teaching useful job skills. Some of the young people in the quilting program spent a year working on a quilt that they presented to Dorothy and me—and we put that up on display at the Patrick Henry building for all to see. We have it at our house in McLean now and it means so much to us.

Dorothy and I had a reception at the mansion for these young people. We were there in the foyer of the mansion, and one young man told me he wanted my job.

"I'm going to be governor," he said. "I'm going to be living here one day."

"You made them feel like people," Andy said. "You believed on a deep level in these kids and believed on a deep level about redemption. You really liked having them around, and you had them come to your cabinet room to talk about student government. You really embraced them, and made them feel like they could write a different story in their lives."

Our reform effort for our juvenile justice system, which saved the state more than $40 million by reducing the population of these facilities, caught the attention of the Annie E. Casey Foundation in Baltimore, which committed $2 million in staff assistance and training. "There are a lot of states that are trying new things," Tom Woods of the foundation told the *Richmond Times-Dispatch*. "I'm not aware of any state moving as intently on as many fronts as Virginia is."

Andy Block's visionary leadership had a huge impact in Virginia and nationally. I love working with energetic people like Andy, who are not afraid to shake it up. You have to empower people. I think of the thousands of people who have worked for me, through the various enterprises and initiatives I've started in business and in politics, and I've always urged them to break through walls and try new things. I've always said, "Think differently and try new things." That's what I'd always tell my cabinet: I will not be disappointed if you try something new and fail, I will only be disappointed if you don't try anything new at all.

I represented eight and a half million people equally, every one of them. The people at the top didn't need my help. I spent my time thinking about the people most in need, many of them in the rural parts of the state who didn't vote for me, but that didn't matter, I was still the leader of their state.

On education, the single most important issue I tackled as governor, I followed a similar approach to our work on juvenile detention, hiring dynamic leaders who could make a difference, starting and ending all policy discussions with an emphasis on taking on disparities and inequities, and making sure through additional funding that there would be resources to help take a major step forward. I was shocked at the different levels of education in different parts of the commonwealth. If you're not giving these kids a great start, they're going to have a bad finish. Every child and young person ought to have access to the same quality education, starting with pre-K, and it was atrocious how far we were from true equity.

"I think a lot of times when people think of education, they think of equal, but equity means that those students who are living in poverty and going to school have the same support as those students in more affluent areas, so that means tutors, breakfast, lunch, dinner, after-school programs, and summer programs," Lamont Bagby, head of the Virginia Legislative Black Caucus, told me. "I think it's important for everyone to have that."

My secretary of education, Anne Holton, and I went on a visit to Petersburg, twenty-five miles south of Richmond, and could not believe what we saw in the schools. There were holes in the walls and holes in the ceilings, and poor, outmoded equipment, no kind of environment for students to get the most out of educational opportunities. It was a vicious cycle. Petersburg is a low-income community, ranking 276 out of 372 communities in Virginia, with a per capita income of $15,989, which meant the district had very little money, since education funding depends on local property tax rates. Petersburg teachers tended to be more junior and lower on the pay scale.

The first step was to improve morale. We had a public event talking about our plans to invest more in education and help districts like Petersburg, which are part of a larger pattern of inequity in education across Virginia and the United States.

"Wait a minute, have you *been* to our schools?" one little boy asked after raising his hand. "Do you know what you're talking about?"

"Yes, we have," I could say. "We know exactly what you're talking about and that's why we want to fix it."

Working in a bipartisan manner with the general assembly, we were able to add money to the budget so that Petersburg could afford to go after a dynamic superintendent. The district lured Marcus J. Newsome away from Chesterfield County, a more affluent area, to take on the challenge of helping Petersburg close the gap.

"It's all about my love and care for children and believing that children in Petersburg deserve a quality education," Newsome told the *Richmond Times-Dispatch*. "And that starts with experienced leadership."

Newsome in turn brought a team of gifted visionaries on education and made an immediate impact. "Getting someone of his commitment and caliber energized the whole community," Anne Holton says.

I was never under any illusions. I knew I wasn't going to solve this all in one go, but I was going to die trying. There's no silver bullet. You attack a problem on as many fronts as possible. "Lots of little things have added up," as Anne put it.

As first lady, Dorothy was nationally recognized for her work to end child hunger by leveraging federal child nutrition programs in schools across Virginia. She worked with local schools and community leaders to increase access to school breakfasts, after-school and summer meals for students in need. We have to ensure every child's most basic needs are met every day in order for them to have a chance to learn and thrive and reach their full potential. "Children can't be hungry for knowledge, if they're just plain hungry," she says. "Understanding and recognizing the pain and suffering so many families are going through is an important step to healing and making life better for all."

We started a new program called Classrooms, Not Courtrooms, so that schools couldn't throw students out onto the street for a week all based on flimsy justification. We helped many schools go from unaccredited to accredited or accredited with conditions, overall a major step forward. We worked hard on filling teacher vacancies and hiring more experienced teachers and made some progress, but as Anne likes to say, it's a long road and progress has to be sustained.

"We didn't go in as Big Brother, we went in saying, 'We have resources and we want to help, how can we help?'" says Dietra Trent, who took over as secretary of education when Anne resigned in 2016 to campaign with her husband, Senator Tim Kaine, Hillary's running mate. "By the time we left, Petersburg was in a much stronger place. They still have challenges, but they are on the road to recovery."

As I said in my final State of the Commonwealth Address in January 2018, "Even in times of fiscal difficulty, we protected K-12 education from budget cuts, and worked together to make the largest investment in education in the history of Virginia. We reformed the standards of learning and eliminated five tests, transformed our workforce training programs, and redesigned our high school curriculum to better align it with the needs of a twenty-first-century economy."

That was an emotional night. I was proud of the progress we'd made in four years, even with a Republican legislature that sometimes worked against me. We'd brought in more than $20 billion in new capital investment during my four years as governor, a record, boosted personal income 12.3 percent, and dropped unemployment from 5.4 percent to 3.6 percent. At the same time, I had only one term, and Virginia state law bars running for successive terms, but I knew there was so much work yet to be done, starting with healing the racial divide in the wake of Charlottesville.

"My final request I would like to leave you with this evening is to please do everything you can to make Virginia a beacon of hope, even in times of fear and hatred," I said. "If restoring Virginians' civil rights was my proudest moment as governor, witnessing the bigotry and violence we saw last August in Charlottesville was the lowest. That day was full of hatred, cowardice, and unspeakable loss. But even in that dark moment, the character that makes this commonwealth great shined through. We saw it in the three Virginians who were taken from us on that terrible day.

"Heather Heyer was a passionate thirty-two-year-old who was on the Downtown Mall on August twelfth fighting for the values that make our commonwealth and our country great. She died fighting for what she believed in, and against hatred and bigotry. When neo-Nazis and white supremacists invaded her community, she stood up and met their hatred with love. Trooper Pilots Jay Cullen and Berke Bates were standing watch from above, protecting the people who participated in the day's events—all of them. They made the ultimate sacrifice doing what so many of their brothers and sisters in law enforcement continue to do every day—upholding the belief that every person should be protected by the law, no matter who they are.

"Nothing will bring these brave Virginians back. But as we continue to mourn their loss, I hope we will honor their legacy by finding the good in each other and in our commonwealth, even in times of great challenge. Tonight we are joined by several people who loved these fine Virginians and miss them every day, as we all do. Won't you please join me in welcoming Heather Heyer's mother, Susan; her stepfather, Kim; Berke Bates's wife, Amanda, and Jay Cullen's wife, Karen, and son Ryan?"

The time for mourning had not yet ended. Charlottesville and what we lost there was a great tragedy. But we had an idea of the direction we had to take to honor that tragedy and honor those lives lost.

A Time for Action

. . .

Two years after Charlottesville, the blunt reality is we find ourselves in danger of not living up to the legacy of that tragic weekend in August 2017. Heather Heyer's mother, Susan Bro, made the point at her daughter's memorial service that the Nazi James Fields tried to silence her daughter with his act of terrorism, weaponizing his car against that crowd of peaceful protesters. "Well, guess what," she said. "You just magnified her." Susan urged everyone inspired by Heather's death, whether they live in Charlottesville or another part of Virginia or anywhere around the world, to use it as an inspiration to get out there and work for change. "You make it happen," she said. "You take that extra step. You find a way to make a difference in the world."

Susan Bro handled the loss of her daughter with great dignity and grace. Since Heather's death she has followed her own advice and gone to work, traveling the country to give talks urging people to get involved and actively work for change and social justice. Saying the right things isn't enough. Action counts. As

Robert F. Kennedy put it, "Progress is a nice word, but change is its motivator. And change has its enemies."

When I talked recently to Susan Bro, looking back on Charlottesville after almost two years, she said she'd like to see more of a sense of urgency from more people. "Heather helped to open my eyes to a lot of things I'd been putting my head in the sand about," Susan told me. "If after Charlottesville we just talk about 'Love one another' and have a kumbaya moment here, then we accomplish nothing, then we're back to square one."

Racism has been deeply ingrained in the fabric of our country throughout our history, and people have tried to shove it under the rug, again and again, citing progress. In Virginia, even with racist symbols all around, and some Virginia license plates still being issued with Confederate flags until I banned the practice, a jolt was needed to move us beyond the genteel sense of complacency. Charlottesville provided more than a jolt. It was a lightning bolt. Charlottesville lit up the scourge of racism and hatred of others as it really is, in the here and now. That spotlight offered an opportunity, but we have only a limited window to use that opportunity to leverage real change.

"If we don't do it now, then we definitely wasted an opportunity—and wasted a life, frankly," Susan told me. "That's what I go around the country telling people."

Then we wasted three lives, I'd say, including my friends Jay Cullen and Berke Bates. But this is larger than three lives and all the lives they touched. This is about all of us, who we are, how we live, and what we tolerate and don't tolerate. This is about what we demand and don't demand, of ourselves and others.

"The focus on Heather has tended to put a white savior complex yet again on black issues," Susan told me. "I've had to be very adamant about pulling back on that and saying, 'No, Heather is just a small part of the story.' This was an awakening for a lot of white people, but black people were already quite well aware of the hateful agendas of some of the hate groups."

That's a point I heard from every African American I talked to about Charlottesville.

"White people are now getting the opportunity to see that we are not a post-racial society, just because President Obama was elected, and this is not just about Trump," Charlottesville City Council member Wes Bellamy told me. "There are a lot of people who practice both covert and overt racism. So what do we do? Do we change policies? Do white people lend their voice as well as their privilege to be able to help out those who are disenfranchised? I think we can do that. . . . A lot of people could take a cue from Governor McAuliffe. He hired the first black secretary of the commonwealth. He restored voting rights. He took action and worked for equality. That's how you use your privilege. That's what you do."

Levar Stoney thinks that after Charlottesville, there is no going back on issues of race. "You know from the history of Virginia that we've been very genteel in our treatment of racism," he said. "We're very passive about it. Like: We're not as bad as Alabama, we're not as bad as Georgia, we're not as bad as Mississippi. But it's baked into our way of life. After Charlottesville, there's an attitude that we're not going to be genteel, we're not going to be passive. We need to be active, not just in dismantling the symbols of racism, but in how we remove inequality from our institutions like education and housing to build a more just and equitable society."

I was frustrated during my time as governor at how much time gets wasted by people who should be working for real change. People love to play small ball. They get caught up in things that just don't matter. I used to sit in my office with Jennie O'Holleran and my policy team, saying, "Honestly, are you serious? Why am

I having to spend my time vetoing ridiculous bills passed by the Republican legislature that would allow guns into emergency shelters, or prevent a baker from selling a cake to a gay couple?" That shocked me. I think back now on all the time that was wasted, and all the work we have to do, but we can never make real progress until a full sense of urgency kicks in.

"White people don't get it," Larry Sabato says. "We don't feel the sting of racism and don't have the history of insult and hurt that African Americans have. Until whites do get it, progress is going to be limited. We'll never make lasting progress if we pretend race isn't still central to many of the problems that bedevil us. Maybe Charlottesville was the shock to the system we all needed to jumpstart real dialogue. Charlottesville ended the myth, or the dream, that racial reconciliation had mainly happened. Race is still a sore subject even in liberal communities like Charlottesville. In America as a whole, racism is woven into the very fabric of our institutions and our economy."

Really, in the end it doesn't matter who was surprised to see such raw racism and hatred on proud display in the streets of Charlottesville that weekend, it matters what we do. Virginia has made progress, but we have a long way to go. Why does Virginia have 378 monuments to the Civil War? Quit worrying about the cost. The cost to society of not removing them is much greater. We're bold and brave enough to get it done. It's time to take action. We have to start by giving local authorities decision-making power over what to do with their monuments and clear the way for action. The bottom line is: Those monuments are just offensive, and there is plenty of room to put them in museums and cemeteries.

"I think that what happened in Charlottesville has really been a catalyst in ways," A. C. Thompson told me. "It was a catalyst for the white supremacist movement to collapse on itself, and a catalyst for Americans to realize they need to be aware of these issues.

A lot of folks knew there were aggressive racists in their community and they didn't say anything about it or do anything about it. Afterward they did speak up, sometimes against people in their family. It activated people in the workplace. It activated people on the campuses. It activated people in politics. It activated law enforcement. I think there are a lot of actions that have sprung from the awful tragedy in Charlottesville."

In some ways Donald Trump has served as an excuse. Having so unfit a figure in the White House has tied us all up in knots, fixated on his latest antics or tweets, his latest self-serving insults or distractions, his latest failure to see beyond his narrow self-interest or that of his family. Everyone gets so riled up all the time talking Trump this, and Trump that; it can be paralyzing for many. Trump is only a part of the bigger problem. Having him out of the White House will be a start—but only a start.

As Congressman John Lewis told me, "It's not enough, but it will be a down payment on moving toward enough. I just think that he's made the country so much worse off when it comes to the issue of building a community, of building a nation that is free. I thought we were on our way down that road, but every now and then there's some force that comes along and arrests that progress."

Visiting John Lewis to talk about Charlottesville, two years later, was a very special moment. His wisdom moved me and I'm very thankful to him for the powerful Foreword he wrote to this book. Talking to John Lewis is like walking through living history—and that was especially true that day. By chance Robert F. Kennedy Jr. stopped by for a picture; he insisted on a photo with the three of us, and it was amazing to step into Congressman Lewis's office. The walls were covered with incredible pictures cataloguing a remarkable life, but there was only one bust in that room: a bust of Robert F. Kennedy, attorney general in his brother Jack Kennedy's administration, fierce fighter for civil rights, father of the man standing next to me. Bobby Kennedy stood for eloquence backed up by action.

"Each time a man stands up for an ideal, or acts to improve the lot of others, or strikes out against injustice, he sends forth a tiny ripple of hope, and crossing each other from a million different centers of energy and daring, those ripples build a current that can sweep down the mightiest walls of oppression and resistance."

Bobby Kennedy was a fighter. John Lewis is a fighter. I'm a fighter. You have to be a fighter and also work for social change. I'm proud of the work we all did in Virginia, starting with restoring the voting rights of all those individuals who had served their time and paid their debt to society and deserved to feel like full citizens again. I'm proud of moving the commonwealth of Virginia forward, socially and economically, of sending the signal to the world that Virginia is for lovers, we're an open and welcoming state with a twenty-first-century economy and a vision of the future.

Our work during my time as governor was a start, but only a start—and we've all been reminded since then how fleeting progress can be. African Americans find blackface to be disgusting and insulting, and they're right. It was a painful episode when the Virginia governor and attorney general were both embroiled in blackface scandals, especially after we'd spent four years moving Virginia forward.

"It makes me sad," John Lewis told me. "I know some people say, 'Well, it was another time, another period, another day, they were much younger.' But we cannot continue. We're in a different world."

Every day we were focused on blackface in Virginia, we were distracted from the work at hand. As John Lewis says, progress was arrested. We have too much work to do to let ourselves be slowed down. We have too many challenges that demand immediate action, from improving the educational opportunities of every young person in this country to generating the good-paying jobs that are the ultimate answer to economic inequality; from helping displaced workers retrain for the twenty-first-century economy to expanding Medicaid and continuing in the decades-long struggle to improve health care in this country. We need fresh energy, not distractions, which is why I'm so excited to see so much engagement among the young and so many smart, dynamic, qualified younger people getting into politics and nonprofit work in a variety of roles.

To bring more people into politics, we have to reach out to them, especially in less affluent communities. The young can't be inspired, and inspire us in turn, if no one gives them a chance. As Lamont Bagby told me: "Those individuals need resources. They need to be able to come down and see the Virginia House of Delegates in action. They need to go to Washington, DC, and see people in action. They just need to be inspired. They inspire us; we need to make sure that they know the opportunities that are before them."

Until every American and every elected official gets out of bed every single day fighting for social justice and equal opportunity, we are failing as a society. Until we get there, it's all just talk. We have to do a better job at home and in our schools, teaching respect and valuing differences and not sugar-coating the past as heritage rather than inherited racism. We have to take away the barriers to success that affect so many in our communities of color. We have to tackle lack of access to quality health care, mass incarceration, disproportionate prison sentencing and mandatory minimums, and the "lock 'em up" mentality. We've got too many African American students going to dilapidated schools with the roofs falling apart. The issues that Barbara Johns fought for in 1951 are still all too prevalent. Infant mortality rates in African American communities, like Milwaukee, are a scandal. We have to get out of the past and move to the future.

"We have to fix the systems that cause the divide," Susan Bro told me. "We have to fix the inequities, or we're going to end up right back in the same place. In education, housing, business loans, we have to undo the wrongs of the past. Somebody might say they want to undo all that, but are they willing to put their kids in a public school? Or are they only willing to say they want to be a part of the process, but only from the outside?"

The truth was revealed in Charlottesville. We are a divided nation today, stuck in the past, racism still rampant. As bad as it might have been, it was under wraps until Donald Trump got elected," Virginia state senator Louise Lucas, who represents Portsmouth, told me. "He tore the lid off of the reservations people had about being open about it."

Lucas, who was born in 1944, also said, "I have not seen so much hate and vitriol in my adult life. I haven't seen so much since the early days of the Civil Rights Movement."

Young people were the key to change then and they can be the key now, she believes.

"We have to stay in the trenches with them, making them feel they are part of the process," she said. "We have to make sure that their active minds have something to think about and their busy hands have something to do. We have to keep them engaged to let them know there is hope, everybody working together, Generation X and Millennials and all generations.

If you were offended, disgusted, and outraged by what happened in Charlottesville, good! Then it's your responsibility to do something about it. Up until Trump, and up until Charlottesville, race was something that, too often, people didn't want to talk about. There was a notion kicking around that we'd corrected the problem. That was false. People felt too comfortable in their insular little worlds.

My message to everybody is: Stop being comfortable. Stop believing we've come so far. As Charlottesville has proven, we haven't. I'd like to thank all the peaceful protesters who came out in Charlottesville to oppose hate. That wasn't comfortable. You won't feel comfortable when you're out there working for change.

You won't feel comfortable taking on hatred and bigotry. Forget reconciliation commissions. Words, words, words. It's a bunch of white people sitting around together trying to feel comfortable to talk a problem to death, but it doesn't bring change. Action brings change. Do something. Do it now.

Acknowledgments

. . .

I want to thank Susan Bro, Heather Heyer's mother, for talking to me repeatedly for this book and making invaluable contributions; and I want to thank Karen Cullen and Amanda Bates, who lost their husbands in the helicopter crash that August 12 and who lent their support to the project, but chose not to be quoted. If you would like to support them, as I am doing with this book, you can donate to the following:

The Heather Heyer Foundation
P.O. Box 7153
Charlottesville, VA 22906
www.heatherheyerfoundation.com;

The Virginia State Police Association
6944 Forest Hill Avenue
Richmond, VA 23225
www.vspa.org/news/news-how-to-donate-to-the-lt-jay-cullens
-and-trooper-pilot-berke-m-m-bates-1/

I also want to thank all my colleagues in Virginia state government who were so helpful with this book project. You know who you are! Special thanks to Brian Moran, Larry Sabato Jr., and Nicky Zamostny, for their patience in answering repeated questions.

Tom Dunne published my first book, *What a Party!*, a *New York Times* bestseller when it came out in 2007, and it was great to work with him again, as well as with our editor Stephen S. Power, assistant editor Samantha Zukergood, publicist Joe Rinaldi and the whole team at Thomas Dunne Books and St. Martin's Press.

Thanks as well to Steve Kettmann, co-director of a writers retreat center in California called the Wellstone Center in the Redwoods and a contriubutor to *The New York Times* and other publications. He helped me write my first book and encouraged me to do this book on Charlottesville, and was with me at every step in the process.

Finally, thanks to my wife Dorothy, my best friend, my partner for thirty years, and the best editor any author could have.

Index

■ ■ ■